P9-DHA-978

Cooking with Caprial

American Bistro Fare

❖ COOKING ❖
WITH CAPRIAL

AMERICAN BISTRO FARE

by Caprial Pence

Ten Speed Press

BERKELEY, CALIFORNIA

For John
My wonderful husband; I will love you forever.

Special Thanks
To the Bistro staff, for all your hard work and support; to my parents, for always supporting me in whatever I set out to do; to my family, for putting up with me and my deadlines; to Chuck, for believing that I could do all this; to Merrilyn, for all the hard work you put into the book; to Ed and Carolyn, for all your help on the photos; and to Clancy, for all your effort—it may have been a rocky road, but we got there.

© 1996 by Caprial Pence
Photographs © 1996 by Edward Gowans
Illustrations © 1996 by Merrilyn Clarke

1☉

Ten Speed Press
P.O. Box 7123
Berkeley, CA 94707

Distributed in Australia by Simon & Schuster Australia; in Canada by Publishers Group West; in New Zealand by Tandem Press; in South Africa by Real Books; in the United Kingdom and Europe by Airlift Books; and in Singapore and Malaysia by Berkeley Books.

Jacket design by Fifth Street Design
Text design by Sarah Levin
Food styling by Carolyn Schirmacher
Jacket photographs by Jerome Hart (front) and
Edward Gowans (back flap and back)
Produced in association with Culinary Arts Television
Printed in Canada

Library of Congress Cataloging in Publication Data
on file with the publisher

    4 5 6 7 8 9 10 —99 98 97

Contents

Introduction

■ When I wrote my last book, *Caprial's Cafe Favorites*, never did I think that so many of you would read the introduction so carefully. I thought that you would be racing through the pages to get to the recipes. While I'm really glad you listened to what I had to say, I am feeling a little pressure with this introduction, now that I know a lot of people will actually read it!

In that introduction, I talked about the tools that you needed to create the recipes contained in the book—basically, a good sharp knife and at least one good ovenproof pan. With these tools, fresh ingredients, and an open mind, you should be ready to roll. Here, I just want to talk about why I cook like I do. So I will try my best in these few paragraphs to impart a bit of what I know and think about food.

With two books behind me, my third television series in production (this time on public television), and my restaurant and cooking classes going strong, I find my days and nights are brimful of two things I love: cooking and teaching. Teaching people about food is great: it is so satisfying to see the gleam in someone's eye when they tell you how well their dinner party turned out—how when they brought out the dessert, everyone oohed and aahed. That kind of story makes me feel terrific. Cooking is such a great source of enjoyment for so many of us, and I hope to add to that enjoyment with the recipes in this book. Until you have spent an afternoon in a cozy kitchen baking fragrant bread, like my Olive Bread or Bistro Challah Bread, you can't know how relaxing it really is.

I would love to teach and help you make a meal where your whole family sits down together for the first time in a long time, or create a dinner to celebrate the holidays or another special event. But I really don't want you to spend hours in the kitchen or running all over town trying to find ingredients. My goal with every recipe I design for you is that it be approachable and make you feel confident about what you are cooking. Don't worry for days about what you are going to cook. If you can't get a specific ingredient, or if you imagine another element that might taste good in a dish, feel free to improvise and substitute! Just enjoy the process of cooking the dish and sharing it with friends and family.

If this book has a culinary theme, it is American bistro fare. So what is that? To me, it's elegant, eclectic food drawn from the world's great cuisines that is simple to prepare and satisfying to eat! I think that we sometimes get so comfortable with what we cook and eat that we can find it hard to break out of that routine. But why should you or I have to stick with the cuisine of one culture exclusively when we have more and more access to the ingredients and cooking techniques not only of France and Italy, but of India and Thailand?

The truth is there's room for well-prepared classics with a twist and new-found favorite flavors in anybody's kitchen. I would hate to be tied down to one way of thinking about food, and I want to expose the readers of my books and the viewers of my television shows to as many new ideas and unexpected flavors as possible—they will only make your cooking richer and more exciting. By designing these recipes with many cultural influences—yet keeping them approachable and easy to prepare—I hope to help people to become more adventurous in their cooking and eating habits. I am proud to say that the theme of this book is, simply, good food.

Let's talk for a minute about the issue of fat in the recipes beyond these pages. Yes, I do use cream and butter. My goal is simply to create recipes that taste good, and I don't mean to imply that because I have two chapters of desserts, I think you should have dessert every night. I am counting on all of you to be sensible about your everyday diet wants and needs, and your lifestyle. Life is about balance: people need to be conscious of what they eat, but that shouldn't mean they can never enjoy a dessert or a pizza with peppers, olives, and feta. To me, never having a piece of chocolate, or even cheese, does not make for a very pleasant way to live. So I am telling you to use these recipes sensibly, and enjoy them without guilt. For most of us, there are many better things to worry about than whether we've had a bite of something with cream in it.

So my advice, as always, is to take this book in your hand, go into your kitchen, and get to work. Remember, I like to see my books open on people's kitchen counters, filled with fingerprints and lots of gooey pages. Celebrate your life by enjoying it with great food.

Portland, Oregon
October, 1995

■ NOTES:

Wherever possible, use fresh herbs—the difference in flavor is truly remarkable. In this book, unless I've specified ground or dried herbs, the quantities I've given are for chopped fresh herbs. If you have to use dried herbs, cut the quantity in half; so 1 teaspoon of fresh chopped basil would be ½ teaspoon of dried basil.

Though international ingredients are increasingly common and indispensable in our kitchens, I've included some of the less common ingredients and terms (along with selected preparation techniques) in the Glossary that follows this introduction. (For British readers, there is also a measurement conversion chart and a list of British terms.)

Glossary

Asian chile sauce A sweet-hot Thai sauce made of chiles, sugar, and vinegar. (I use Mae Paoy brand in the restaurant.) Available in specialty markets.

blanch To boil rapidly and very briefly in a lot of water.

bok choy and baby bok choy Also called Chinese white cabbage, bok choy is a dark green cabbage that somewhat resembles Swiss chard; baby bok choy is a smaller, more tender variety

butterfly To cut a piece of meat nearly all the way through and open it out to make it twice as long but half as thick as it was. The meat should then be pounded flat with a meat mallet.

caramelize With sugar, to cook over heat until brown to enrich the flavor. With meat and vegetables, to cook over high heat to bring out and brown the natural sugars, adding an intensity of flavor.

chile paste A Chinese condiment made from fermented fava beans, red chiles, and, sometimes, garlic.

chorizo sausage A spicy Mexican sausage made with pork and beef and seasoned with chile. Available in specialty markets and many supermarkets.

coddle To pour boiling water over eggs, allowing them to stand briefly before removing.

crystallized ginger Also known as candied ginger. Available in most supermarkets.

daikon radish A long, white, Asian radish shaped like a carrot. It is hot when not peeled and mild when peeled. Available in many supermarkets.

debeard For mussels: to scrape away the "beard" on the shell. Mussels should be very well scrubbed and debearded before use. Do not use any mussels with open shells.

fermented black beans Small black soybeans that are cooked and fermented with salt and spices. Widely used in Chinese cooking, and available in specialty markets and some supermarkets.

five-spice powder An ancient Chinese spice mixture of star anise, fennel (anise seed), cloves, cinnamon, and Sichuan peppercorns. Some brands include citrus peel or cardamom as well. Strong, hot, fragrant, and slightly sweet, a little of this powder goes a long way. Available in specialty markets and most supermarkets.

génoise A sponge cake containing butter and leavened with stiffly beaten eggs.

gravlax Scandinavian cured salmon (usually cured with salt, pepper, dill, and aquavit).

hoisin sauce A rich brownish red Asian sauce made from soybean paste, garlic, vinegar, sugar, and spices. Available in specialty markets and some supermarkets.

hot-smoked salmon Salmon that is cooked as well as smoked (as opposed to cold-smoked salmon—like lox—which is smoked but not cooked).

Italian plums Large fresh prunes.

kalamata olives Smooth, purple, brine-cured Greek olives with an intense aftertaste. Usually packed in vinegar, and available in specialty markets and many supermarkets.

kosher salt   Pure salt with an even, coarse texture; more soluble than table salt. Available in specialty markets and most supermarkets.

lemongrass   A standard herb in Vietnamese and Thai cooking. Use fresh lemongrass for cooking; dried lemongrass is mainly used for tea. Available in specialty markets and some supermarkets.

mesclun   Mixed wild greens.

Mexican cocoa powder   Powder made from cinnamon, vanilla, sweet chocolate, sugar, and almonds. Ibarra is the most widely available brand. Available in specialty markets and some supermarkets.

mirin wine   Sweet Japanese wine made from glutinous rice; has a low alcohol content.

nonreactive bowl   A glass, ceramic, or stainless steel bowl, not an aluminum or cast-iron one. It's important to use only nonreactive containers when preparing and storing dishes, such as dressings or marinades, which contain acidic ingredients such as vinegar or lemon juice.

oyster sauce   A staple condiment of Chinese cooking, this rich brown sauce is made with oysters, soy sauce, salt, and spices. The fishy taste abates in the brewing process. Be aware that cheaper brands may have MSG and other additives. Available in specialty markets and some supermarkets.

palm sugar   Dark brown sugar made from the sap of palm trees; available in solid block form. Dark brown cane sugar can be substituted if you cannot find palm sugar.

pancetta   Unsmoked, peppered Italian bacon. Available in specialty markets and in some supermarkets.

pepper bacon   Bacon with a peppered crust.

prosciutto   Dry-cured spiced Italian ham. Available in specialty markets.

reduce   To thicken and intensify the flavor of a liquid by evaporating it through boiling.

sabayon   Also known as zabaglione. A whipped custard of egg yolks, sugar, and sweet wine.

seasoned rice vinegar   A clear and mild vinegar widely used in Asian cooking. Available in specialty stores and many supermarkets. Cider vinegar can be substituted if necessary.

sesame oil   Available either in light or dark (toasted) varieties. Because of its strong flavor and low burning temperature, it is used as a seasoning rather than as a cooking oil. Available in supermarkets.

shock   To douse quickly in ice-cold water to stop cooking process.

Sichuan peppercorns   One of the five spices in five-spice powder. Reddish-brown in color and less hot than black peppercorns. Available in specialty markets and some supermarkets.

sweat   To cover an ingredient with liquid and barely simmer it to bring out its flavor.

sweet onion   Sweet varieties, such as Walla Walla onions, are usually available in early summer.

tapenade   A thick paste made from capers, anchovies, black olives, olive oil, and lemon juice.

wasabi   Japanese green mustard; similar in flavor and use to horseradish, wasabi is very hot and pungent, and should be used sparingly. Available in powder and paste form in specialty markets and increasingly in supermarkets.

APPETIZERS

Grilled Artichoke Hearts with Garlic and Green Peppercorns

Serves 4

■ This can be served as an appetizer or even as a side dish for a barbecue dinner. Or serve it on an antipasto plate with cheese, roasted garlic, and roasted red peppers with some good crusty Italian bread for a light luncheon.

12 fresh or canned (water-packed) artichoke hearts (cooked if fresh)
¼ cup unsalted butter
6 cloves roasted garlic (see page 198)
1 clove garlic, chopped
Dash white wine
1 teaspoon green peppercorns
Salt and black pepper to taste

Light coals or start grill. Divide the artichoke hearts among 4 skewers.

In a small saucepan, place butter, roasted garlic, fresh garlic, wine, and peppercorns. Bring to a boil over medium heat. Season with salt and pepper.

Place the skewered artichoke hearts on the grill and baste with the butter mixture. Do not overbaste or the fire will flare up and burn the hearts. These are best grilled over low coals to prevent burning. Grill for 2 to 3 minutes on each side. Serve warm or at room temperature, using the leftover butter as a dipping sauce, if you like.

◆▪ Chilled Pear Curry Mussels ▪◆

Serves 6

■ We serve these mussels at the restaurant as an appetizer, but a lot of people pair them with a green salad for lunch or a light dinner. They make an excellent beginning to a meal of Roasted Duck Legs with Wild Rice Pancakes. Finish with Grilled Banana Compote.

2 teapoons vegetable oil
3 cloves garlic, chopped
1 tablespoon chopped gingerroot
1 medium onion, diced
1 tablespoon curry powder
2 pears, peeled, cored, and diced
½ cup apple juice
¼ cup seasoned rice vinegar
1 tablespoon Asian chile sauce
5 pounds mussels, scrubbed and debearded (see Glossary)

Heat oil in a large sauté pan. Add garlic, gingerroot, and onion, and sauté until you can smell the aroma, 1 or 2 minutes. Add curry powder and sauté 1 minute. Add diced pear and apple juice and cook until the pear is tender. Add vinegar and chile sauce. Let cool.

In a second large sauté pan, cook mussels, covered, over high heat until they open, 3 to 5 minutes. Discard any that do not open. Remove mussels from pan, place in a large bowl, and top with cool curry sauce. Chill for about 30 minutes before serving. You may also serve these mussels hot.

◆▪ Grilled Shrimp ▪◆
with Peanut Sauce

Serves 6

▪ Make the peanut sauce early and set aside in the refrigerator until you are ready to serve (it keeps for two weeks). Serve the shrimp hot off the grill, chilled, or at room temperature. You can substitute vegetables for the shrimp if you like. This is a great appetizer to serve to a large group.

▪ PEANUT SAUCE
1 teaspoon chopped gingerroot
1 teaspoon chopped cilantro
1 fresh jalapeño, chopped
¼ cup red wine vinegar
¼ cup soy sauce
Heaping ½ cup creamy peanut butter
1 teaspoon curry powder
1 teaspoon dark sesame oil

▪ GRILLED SHRIMP
16–20 large shrimp, peeled and deveined
1 tablespoon vegetable oil
Salt and black pepper to taste

For the peanut sauce, place gingerroot, cilantro, and jalapeño in a food processor and process until smooth. Add vinegar, soy sauce, and peanut butter and purée until smooth and creamy. Add curry powder and sesame oil. Process until mixed well. Remove from processor and refrigerate until ready to use.

For the shrimp, light coals or start grill. Place peeled shrimp in a bowl, toss with oil, and season with salt and pepper. You may skewer them if you like. When the grill is hot, place shrimp on grill and cook just until they turn pink, 1 to 2 minutes on each side. Remove and place on a tray with the peanut sauce in a small dish on the side.

Oysters on the Half Shell ◆ with Five-Spice Mignonette

Serves 6

■ Use this sauce sparingly: it is very strong! If you are serving these at a party, you can open the oysters one hour ahead of time, then cover them with damp paper towels and place in the refrigerator. Get the freshest oysters you can buy; I always suggest the smaller oysters—they are much nicer.

½ cup dry white wine
¼ cup seasoned rice vinegar
1 large shallot, chopped
2 cloves garlic, chopped
1 teaspoon chopped gingerroot
¼ teaspoon five-spice powder
Pinch chile flakes
36 fresh oysters

For the mignonette, combine wine, vinegar, shallot, garlic, gingerroot, five-spice powder, and chile flakes in a small saucepan and bring to a boil over high heat. Remove from heat and allow to cool.

For the oysters, shuck oysters and either spoon ½ teaspoon of the mignonette over the top of each oyster or serve the mignonette on the side. The oysters are best when served on a bed of crushed ice.

♦♦ Savory Mushroom Cheesecake ♦♦

Serves 12

■ This is a rich appetizer, so make sure that you cut it into small slices. I like to serve it slightly warm, with a bit of Roasted Pepper Salsa on the side to add some tang to the dish.

> 1 tablespoon olive oil
> 1 cup quartered domestic mushrooms
> ½ cup sliced fresh shiitake mushrooms
> 3 shallots, chopped
> 1 head roasted garlic (see page 198)
> ½ cup chopped sun-dried tomatoes
> 10 spinach leaves, stems trimmed
> 1 pound cream cheese
> 3 eggs
> Zest of 1 lemon
> Salt and black pepper to taste

Preheat oven to 350°. Heat oil in a large sauté pan until very hot. Add mushrooms and sauté for 3 to 4 minutes. Add shallots, garlic, tomatoes, and spinach and sauté just until the spinach wilts. Remove from the heat and allow to cool. Cut cream cheese into small cubes and place, along with the eggs and lemon zest, in a food processor. Blend until smooth, stopping to scrape down the sides every so often. Pour mixture into a medium-size bowl and fold in the cooled mushroom mixture. Season with salt and pepper. Place in a greased 9-inch cake pan.

Bake for 30 to 45 minutes, or until a knife inserted in the center comes out clean. Remove from the oven and let cool for 10 to 15 minutes, then invert pan onto a serving plate and remove. Serve warm.

Smoked Chicken Curry Turnovers

Makes 6 entrees or 18 appetizers

■ If you can't find smoked chicken or you don't have time to smoke your own (see page 195), then just use roasted or even poached chicken. You can make the turnovers ahead and freeze, then pull out when you are ready to serve—you don't even have to thaw them out before baking.

■ CURRY SAUCE
½ cup apple juice
½ cup dry sherry
½ cup white wine
2 shallots, chopped
3 cloves garlic, chopped
2 cups heavy cream
1 tablespoon curry powder
Salt and black pepper to taste

■ TURNOVERS
1 smoked chicken breast, julienned
1 pear, peeled, cored, and sliced
1 red bell pepper, diced
1 small sweet onion, diced
4 ounces fresh mild goat cheese
2 8-by-10-inch sheets Quick Puff Pastry (see page 202),
　　about ⅛-inch thick
Egg wash (1 egg, lightly beaten with 1 tablespoon water)

For the sauce, place the apple juice, sherry, white wine, shallots, and garlic in a medium-size saucepan. Boil over high heat to reduce until about ¼ cup of liquid remains. Add cream and reduce until about 1¼ cups of liquid remain. Heat a small sauté pan until hot. Add the curry powder and heat, stirring, until you smell the aroma, about 1 minute. Add curry powder to sauce and season with salt and pepper. Allow to cool.

For the turnovers, preheat oven to 425°. Place chicken, pear, pepper, onion, goat cheese, and cooled curry sauce in a medium-size bowl. Mix well.

Cut puff pastry into either 18 small squares or 6 large squares. Place an appropriate amount of chicken mixture, depending on the size of the square, on one side of each square. Paint edges of pastry with egg wash. Fold pastry over to form a triangle. Crimp with a fork. Brush tops of the triangles with a bit of egg wash and place on a greased baking sheet. Bake for 15 to 25 minutes, or until golden brown. Serve warm or cold.

Marinated Goat Cheese Rounds with Crostini

Serves 6

■ This is a simple appetizer that is meant to be eaten at leisure with a glass of great wine and a group of friends. Sometimes all I need is this appetizer, wine, friends, and a sunny evening on our deck. You can make crostini out of day-old bread, and you can use any flavor of bread you like, but don't make them too far ahead; they are best served warm.

■ MARINATED GOAT CHEESE ROUNDS
6 ounces fresh, soft goat cheese
3 tablespoons balsamic vinegar
2 cloves garlic, chopped
1 tablespoon chopped fresh thyme
1 teaspoon cracked black pepper
10 cured green olives, pitted and coarsely chopped
⅓ cup extra-virgin olive oil

■ CROSTINI
9 ½-inch-thick slices good-quality French bread
2 tablespoons olive oil
1 teaspoon minced garlic

For the goat cheese rounds, roll the cheese into a 4-inch-long log. Slice into 1-inch-thick rounds and place in a shallow dish. In a small bowl, whisk together vinegar, garlic, thyme, pepper, olives, and olive oil until well blended. Pour over the goat cheese and marinate, refrigerated, for 2 hours to 1 week. Before serving, let warm to room temperature, about 30 minutes.

For the crostini, preheat broiler or grill. Drizzle the bread with olive oil, and grill or broil until golden brown. When the crostini come out of the oven or off the grill, rub them with a bit of the minced garlic. Then cut in half on the diagonal. Serve the warm crostini with the goat cheese.

◆ ◆ Asian-Style Gravlax ◆ ◆

Serves 6

■ This is an appetizer that we serve at the restaurant. We accompany it with Ginger, Carrot, and Daikon Salad and wasabi crème fraîche. Be sure to slice the salmon as thin as possible when you serve it.

> 1½ pounds salmon fillets (skin on)
> 2 tablespoons kosher salt
> ¼ cup brown sugar
> ½ teaspoon chile flakes
> ½ teaspoon five-spice powder
> ½ cup peeled, thinly sliced gingerroot

Place the salmon on a baking sheet. In a small bowl, combine salt, sugar, chile flakes, and five-spice powder. Mix well. Spread the gingerroot over top and bottom of the salmon. Cover salmon with spice mixture on both sides. Cover with plastic wrap and refrigerate for 3 days, or until the fish is firm to the touch.

To serve, slice the salmon as thinly as you can with a very sharp knife. Serve cold with French bread and crème fraîche mixed with wasabi paste.

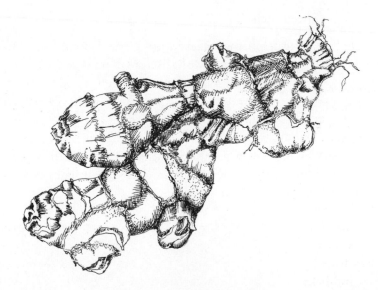

Scallop Seviche
with Cumin Baked Tortilla Chips

Serves 4

■ I like to serve this on a summer evening on our deck. When you bake your own chips, you lower the fat. It is best to let the seviche marinate overnight so that the citrus juice can "cook" the scallops. (Pictured opposite page 6.)

■ SCALLOP SEVICHE
1½ pounds sea scallops, sliced
1 red bell pepper, finely diced
1 small red onion, minced
3 cloves garlic, chopped
1 teaspoon chopped gingerroot
Juice of 1 lime
Zest of 1 lime
Juice of 1 lemon
Zest of 1 lemon
2 tablespoons rice vinegar
¼ cup olive oil
½ teaspoon chile powder
½ teaspoon ground cumin
Salt and black pepper to taste

■ CUMIN BAKED TORTILLA CHIPS
8 large flour tortillas
2 teaspoons ground cumin
1 large dried ancho pepper, oven roasted then pulverized (see page 200)
2 teaspoons kosher salt

For the seviche, place scallops in a nonreactive bowl, add diced pepper and onion, and mix. In a medium-size bowl mix garlic, gingerroot, citrus juice, zest, and vinegar. Slowly whisk in olive oil. Season with chile powder, cumin, salt, and pepper and mix. Refrigerate for at least 6 hours or overnight.

For the tortilla chips, preheat oven to 375°. Lightly grease a large baking sheet. Cut the tortillas into 8 wedges. Lay them in one layer on the baking sheet. In a small bowl, mix together cumin, ancho pepper, and salt. Sprinkle the spice mixture over the chips and bake for 6 to 10 minutes, or until golden brown. Remove from pan and cool. You may need to bake the chips in more than one batch. Serve chips with chilled seviche.

◆ Seared Scallops ◆
with Spicy Green Sauce

Serves 4

■ Make the sauce before you cook the scallops. Be careful not to overcook the scallops—you want them to just melt in your mouth. You can make this sauce more or less spicy, as your preference dictates, by increasing or decreasing the amount of chile sauce. Serve on a bed of egg noodles or steamed rice.

■ SPICY GREEN SAUCE

2 cloves garlic, chopped
1 tablespoon chopped gingerroot
2 green onions, chopped
¼ cup packed fresh basil leaves
1 cup spinach leaves
1 teaspoon orange juice concentrate
1 teaspoon palm sugar or brown sugar
¼ cup seasoned rice vinegar
2 tablespoons hoisin sauce
1 tablespoon oyster sauce
2 tablespoons Asian chile sauce
1 tablespoon dark sesame oil

■ SEARED SCALLOPS

1 cup flour
1 tablespoon five-spice powder
2 tablespoons sesame seeds
1½ pounds sea scallops
1 tablespoon olive oil

For the sauce, place garlic, gingerroot, green onions, basil, and spinach in a food processor and blend until smooth. Add orange juice concentrate, palm sugar, vinegar, hoisin sauce, oyster sauce, chile sauce, and sesame oil and process until smooth. Set aside while preparing the scallops.

For the scallops, place flour, five-spice powder, and sesame seeds in a bowl and mix well. If the scallops are very large, you may want to cut them in half. In a large sauté pan, heat olive oil until smoking hot. Place scallops in hot pan over high heat and sear on both sides, about 2 minutes per side. Remove from pan and serve with spicy green sauce and steamed rice or noodles.

Skewered Mushrooms ◆ with Roasted Garlic Sauce

Serves 6

■ If you are serving these for a party, you can get them ready the night before or earlier that day. Then all you have to do is grill them at the last minute and serve them warm to your guests. The garlic sauce also makes a great spread for sandwiches, instead of mayonnaise, and it's even better on hamburgers.

■ ROASTED GARLIC SAUCE
5 heads roasted garlic (see page 198)
2 tablespoons balsamic vinegar
⅓ cup sour cream
1 tablespoon chopped fresh basil
1 teaspoon chopped fresh thyme
1 teaspoon prepared horseradish
Salt and black pepper to taste

■ MUSHROOMS
36 medium-size mushrooms
2 tablespoons balsamic vinegar
¼ cup olive oil
Salt and black pepper to taste

For garlic sauce, remove the roasted garlic cloves from their hulls and place in a food processor. Purée, then add vinegar, sour cream, basil, thyme, and horseradish, and process to blend. Season with salt and pepper. Set aside in refrigerator until ready to use.

For the mushrooms, place mushrooms in a bowl and add vinegar, oil, salt, and pepper. Toss well. Skewer 3 mushrooms apiece on medium-size skewers. Light coals or heat grill. Grill mushrooms for 2 to 3 minutes on each side. Serve warm with roasted garlic sauce.

Broiled Oysters
with Roasted Jalapeño Purée

Serves 4

■ The jalapeño purée in this dish is hot; just a bit goes a long way. Combine five or six different appetizers for a fun way to serve people at a dinner party. Then finish with a couple of desserts, such as Puff Pastry Fruit Tart or Chocolate Truffle Tart.

6 large fresh jalapeños, roasted, peeled,
    and seeded (see page 200)
1 clove garlic, chopped
Pinch chile powder
½ teaspoon ground cumin
½ teaspoon chopped cilantro
3 tablespoons vegetable oil
Salt to taste
16 fresh oysters, shucked

Place peppers, garlic, chile powder, cumin, and cilantro in a food processor and process until smooth. Add oil and salt and process to mix. Set aside until ready to use.

Preheat broiler. Place oysters on a baking sheet and top with just a bit of the purée, less than ½ teaspoon. Broil oysters for 3 to 5 minutes, depending on their size, until plump. Serve hot with more of the jalapeño purée, if you like, or with lemon wedges.

Smoked Trout Napoleons

Serves 6

■ This is a very elegant appetizer. Serve these napoleons with champagne at midnight on January First—a great way to toast the New Year.

    1 sheet Quick Puff Pastry (see page 202), 9 by 11 inches
    6 ounces cream cheese
    2 cloves garlic, chopped
    1 tablespoon lemon juice
    1 teaspoon chopped fresh dill
    ½ teaspoon chopped fresh thyme
    1 pound smoked boneless trout
    ¼ pound arugula
    1 large vine-ripened tomato, seeded and chopped
    1 small cucumber, peeled, seeded, and diced

Preheat oven to 375°. Place puff pastry on a baking sheet and bake until golden brown, about 20 minutes. Remove from oven and allow to cool for about 10 minutes.

When cool, place pastry on a cutting board and cut in half lengthwise and then into thirds crosswise. Split each of the pieces in half and set aside.

In a food processor or mixer bowl, place cream cheese, garlic, lemon juice, dill, and thyme. Process until cream cheese is softened.

Take the bottom of each piece of pastry and spread about 2 tablespoons of the cream cheese mixture gently on each piece. Distribute the smoked trout among the 6 pieces, then arrange the arugula on top of the trout. Top the arugula with chopped tomato and cucumber, then place a pastry top on each piece. Serve immediately.

Goat Cheese Dumplings

Serves 6

■ This is a simple but delightful appetizer. It is both crispy and tender, and filled with cheese. These dumplings are great with wine before dinner.

> ¾ cup soft, fresh goat cheese
> 2 cloves garlic, chopped
> 1 head roasted garlic (see page 198)
> 1 tablespoon chopped fresh basil
> 1 red bell pepper, roasted, peeled, seeded and diced (see page 200)
> Salt and black pepper to taste
> 12 wonton wrappers
> 4 cups vegetable oil, for deep-frying

Place goat cheese in a medium-size bowl. Add garlic, roasted garlic, basil, and roasted red pepper and mix well. Season with salt and pepper and mix.

Place 1 tablespoon of this mixture in the middle of a wonton wrapper. Fold both ends in toward the middle. Then fold one side over to meet the other and roll to resemble an egg roll. Seal the end of the dumpling with water. Repeat with the rest of the wrappers.

Heat oil in a medium-size saucepan until hot. Place a few of the dumplings in the hot oil (don't crowd them) and cook until golden brown, 3 to 4 minutes. Drain dumplings on paper towels while you cook the rest. Serve dumplings warm.

◆◆ Crispy Lamb Dumplings ◆◆

Serves 6

■ This is a great party appetizer. You can wrap the dumplings a day or even a week ahead and freeze them, then just fry and serve. I like to serve them with a sweet-hot Thai sauce that we buy for the restaurant.

4 cups plus 1 teaspoon vegetable oil
2 cloves garlic, chopped
2 teaspoons chopped gingerroot
1 pound ground lamb
2 tablespoons hoisin sauce
½ teaspoon Asian chile sauce, plus additional for dipping
2 green onions, minced
Soy sauce to taste
18 round wonton wrappers

In a medium sauté pan, heat 1 teaspoon oil until very hot. Add garlic and ginger-root and sauté until you can smell the aroma. Add lamb and cook until it is cooked through. Add hoisin sauce and chile sauce and mix. Remove from heat and allow to cool. Mix in onions and season with soy sauce.

To assemble, place 1 tablespoon of lamb mixture in the middle of a wonton wrapper. Brush a bit of water around the edge and fold over to form a half-circle. Crimp the edge and set aside. Continue the process until all the wrappers have been filled.

Heat 4 cups oil in a medium-size saucepan until very hot. Place as many dumplings in the pan as will fit and cook on both sides until golden brown, about 2 to 3 minutes. Drain on paper towels while you cook the rest of the dumplings. Serve warm with a bit of the chile sauce for dipping.

◆•. Panfried Ravioli ◆•
with Roasted Red Pepper Pesto

Serves 4

■ We have been serving these raviolis since almost the day we opened the restaurant, and it is still the most popular recipe we have come up with. If we ever thought about taking these off the menu we would be in a whole lot of trouble. Be sure to use fresh ravioli—the packaged kind does not work here.

■ ROASTED RED PEPPER PESTO
3 red bell peppers, roasted, peeled, and seeded (see page 200)
2 cloves garlic, chopped
½ cup toasted walnuts
½ cup grated Parmesan cheese
⅓ cup olive oil
2 teaspoons chopped fresh basil
Salt and black pepper to taste

■ RAVIOLI
2 tablespoons olive oil
16 fresh ravioli
¼ cup grated Parmesan cheese

For the pesto, in a food processor place peppers, garlic, and walnuts and process until roughly chopped. Add Parmesan cheese and process. With the motor running, slowly drizzle in the oil. Add basil. Season the mixture with salt and pepper and mix again. Set aside.

For the ravioli, heat oil in a large sauté pan until very hot. Add ravioli and cook until golden brown on both sides. Place on plates and top with roasted red pepper pesto and Parmesan cheese.

Crab Bruschetta

Serves 4

■ Bruschetta is basically toast: what makes this dish great is the crab topping. Don't put the crab on top of the toast too soon or the bruschetta will become soggy.

   4 large slices French bread
   ¼ cup plus 2 teaspoons olive oil
   ⅔ cup crabmeat
   2 cloves garlic, chopped
   1 red onion, diced
   1 large plum tomato, diced
   2 tablespoons lemon juice
   Zest of 1 lemon
   ½ teaspoon chopped fresh tarragon
   Salt and cracked black pepper to taste

Brush slices of French bread with 2 teaspoons oil. Toast under a broiler or in oven until golden brown. In a medium-size bowl, combine crabmeat, garlic, red onion, and tomato. In a small bowl, whisk lemon juice, lemon zest, tarragon, and ¼ cup olive oil. Season with salt and cracked black pepper. Add to crab mixture and mix well. Top each of the slices of bread with a quarter of the mixture. Serve immediately.

Vegetable Phyllo Pockets

Serves 6

■ If you like, make these pockets bigger and serve them as a vegetarian entrée instead of as an appetizer. Try other vegetables in the mixture, maybe some chopped cured olives. You can also freeze these before baking them.

■ FILLING

2 teaspoons olive oil
1 small onion, diced
3 cloves garlic, chopped
1 small zucchini, diced
½ cup sliced wild mushrooms or domestic mushrooms
1 red bell pepper, roasted, peeled, seeded, and diced (see page 200)
¼ cup grated Parmesan cheese
¼ cup ricotta cheese
2 teaspoons diced sun-dried tomatoes
1 teaspoon fresh thyme
½ teaspoon cracked black pepper
Salt to taste

■ TO ASSEMBLE

1 tablespoon unsalted butter, melted
6 sheets phyllo dough

For the filling, in a large sauté pan heat olive oil until very hot. Add onions and garlic and sauté until you can smell the aroma. Add zucchini and mushrooms and sauté until crisp-tender, about 3 minutes. Add peppers and mix well. Remove from heat and allow to cool. Add Parmesan, ricotta cheese, sun-dried tomatoes, thyme, and pepper and mix well. Season with salt and set aside.

To assemble the pockets, preheat oven to 350°. Lay the sheets of phyllo out on a board and cut in half crosswise. Stack the sheets on top of one another and set to the side. Place 1 half-sheet on a board and brush with some of the melted butter. Top with another half-sheet of phyllo and brush with more butter. Place about a sixth of the filling mixture in the middle of the bottom half of the phyllo. Fold the sides of the phyllo over the mixture, then roll the phyllo up to resemble an egg roll. Brush with butter and place on a baking sheet. Repeat with remaining phyllo and filling.

Bake for 20 to 30 minutes, or until golden brown. Remove from the oven and cool for a few minutes. Serve warm.

Warm Seafood Mousse
with Fennel Salsa

Serves 6

■ When you are putting this mousse together, it is very important that everything be very cold, including the food processor bowl. This will keep the mousse from separating. Also, be careful not to overprocess the mousse, as this will also cause it to get too warm and separate. (Pictured opposite page 7.)

■ FENNEL SALSA
2 teaspoons olive oil
1 medium fennel bulb, diced
    (reserve green top for garnish)
3 cloves garlic, chopped
2 shallots, chopped
2 tablespoons white wine vinegar
2 medium tomatoes, seeded and diced
¼ cup extra-virgin olive oil
Salt and black pepper to taste

■ SEAFOOD MOUSSE
1 pound white fish fillets, such as cod
1 pound sea scallops
2 cloves garlic, chopped
2 shallots, chopped
1½ cups heavy cream
Salt and black pepper to taste

For the salsa, heat the 2 teaspoons olive oil in a large sauté pan until very hot. Add fennel, garlic, and shallots and sauté until you can smell the aroma of the garlic. Add vinegar and remove from heat. Add tomatoes and mix well. Add the ¼ cup extra-virgin olive oil, and season with salt and pepper. Set aside.

For the mousse, preheat oven to 350°. Dice fish and place in food processor. Add scallops, garlic, and shallots and process until puréed. Scrape down the sides and add cream. Process until smooth and creamy. Season with salt and pepper.

Divide mixture among six 8-ounce greased ramekins. Place in a roasting pan, then fill the pan with water about halfway up the sides of the ramekins. Bake for 30 to 40 minutes, or until a knife inserted in the center comes out clean.

Remove from oven and cool for 2 minutes, then invert each ramekin onto a small plate. Top with the fennel salsa and garnish with a bit of the fennel greens. Serve warm.

◆ Panfried Fresh Mozzarella ◆
with Herb Lemon Sauce

Serves 6

■ We served this appetizer for a wine-tasting dinner at the restaurant. It was delicious paired with a crisp pinot gris. Don't let this get cold, or the cheese will get rubbery.

■ HERB LEMON SAUCE
½ cup unsalted butter
2 shallots, chopped
3 cloves garlic, chopped
½ teaspoon chopped fresh basil
½ teaspoon chopped fresh thyme
½ teaspoon fresh marjoram
Juice of 1 lemon
Salt and black pepper to taste

■ PANFRIED FRESH MOZZARELLA
1½ cups fresh bread crumbs
2 cloves garlic
2 tablespoons Dijon-style mustard
Pinch black pepper
2 eggs, lightly beaten with 2 tablespoons water
6 slices fresh mozzarella cheese (2 ounces each)
1 tablespoon olive oil

For the sauce, place butter in a medium-size sauté pan and bring to a boil over high heat. Add shallots, garlic, basil, thyme, and marjoram. Stir in lemon juice, salt, and pepper. Keep sauce warm while preparing cheese.

For the cheese, place bread crumbs, garlic, mustard, and pepper in bowl of food processor, and process until mixture is smooth. Dredge cheese in egg mixture and then in bread crumb mixture. Set aside.

Heat olive oil in a large sauté pan until smoking hot. Add the breaded cheese slices and brown well on each side, 2 to 3 minutes per side. Remove cheese from pan and place on a tray. Pour herb lemon sauce over cheese and serve hot.

◆▪ Ancho Barbecued ▪◆
Chicken Wings

Serves 6

■ This is a fun appetizer for a large party. Make sure you have lots of napkins around because these are a little messy. Make the sauce spicier if you like. You can make these wings ahead and reheat them before serving.

> ■ ANCHO BARBECUE SAUCE
> 1 teaspoon olive oil
> 1 small onion, minced
> 2 cloves garlic, chopped
> ¾ cup tomato purée
> 4 dried ancho peppers, roasted and pulverized (see page 200)
> ¼ cup hoisin sauce
> 2 tablespoons cayenne sauce
> 1 teaspoon ground cumin
> ¼ teaspoon chile powder
> ½ teaspoon cracked black pepper
> Salt to taste
> ■ CHICKEN WINGS
> 18 chicken wings or drumettes
> Salt and black pepper to taste

For the sauce, heat olive oil in a saucepan until very hot. Add onion and garlic and sauté until you can smell the aroma. Add tomato purée and simmer over low heat for about 2 minutes. Add peppers, hoisin, cayenne sauce, cumin, chile powder, and pepper and simmer for about 5 minutes, stirring often. Season with salt and set aside.

For the chicken, preheat oven to 350°. Place wings or drumettes on a baking sheet and season with salt and pepper. Bake for about 5 to 10 minutes. After 10 minutes, brush generously with barbecue sauce. Bake for another 10 minutes, until chicken is tender. Serve warm.

✚❖ Cheese Ravioli with Tomato Broth ❖✚

Serves 8 as an appetizer, 4 as an entree

■ This can be served as an appetizer or an entree. Make this dish when the tomatoes are very ripe and full of flavor. I like to use yellow tomatoes; they are sweeter than red ones. Serve this in a soup plate, since the sauce is thin.

■ **CHEESE RAVIOLI**

¾ cup ricotta cheese
¼ cup grated Parmesan cheese
¼ cup soft, fresh goat cheese
2 cloves garlic, chopped
Salt and black pepper to taste
8 4 by 4-inch squares fresh pasta

■ **TOMATO BROTH**

2 teaspoons olive oil
3 cloves garlic, chopped
3 shallots, chopped
½ cup red wine
1½ cups Chicken Stock (see page 196) or strong broth
4 very ripe tomatoes, seeded and chopped
2 tablespoons minced sun-dried tomatoes
1 tablespoon chopped fresh basil
½ teaspoon cracked black pepper
Salt to taste

■ **TO ASSEMBLE**

⅓ cup grated Parmesan cheese

For the ravioli, in a small bowl mix together ricotta cheese, Parmesan cheese, goat cheese, and garlic; mix well. Season with salt and pepper and mix well.

Lay 4 of the squares of pasta out on a board and moisten the edges well with water. Place about ¼ cup of the cheese mixture in the middle of each square of pasta, then top with a second pasta square and crimp the edges well. Set aside.

For the tomato broth, heat olive oil in a large sauté pan until very hot. Add garlic and shallots and sauté about 1 minute. Add wine and boil to reduce until almost dry, about 3 minutes. Add chicken stock and ripe tomatoes and reduce over high heat for about 5 minutes. Add sun-dried tomatoes, basil, and pepper and simmer for about 2 minutes. Season with salt. Keep warm.

To assemble, bring 2 quarts of salted water to a boil, add ravioli, and just return water to a boil, 2 to 3 minutes. Divide ravioli among 4 soup plates, then pour tomato broth over them. Serve hot, with Parmesan cheese.

BREADS & SIDES

◆◆ Rosemary French Bread ◆◆

Makes 2 loaves

■ I know, I know: who has time to make bread? Well, I tell you there is nothing like spending a chilly winter afternoon in a cozy kitchen with the smells of rosemary and fresh bread. Talk about a wonderful way to relax.

> 1½ tablespoons active dry yeast
> 2 cups warm water, about 100° to 110°
> 1 tablespoon sugar
> 2 tablespoons chopped fresh rosemary
> 5 cups flour
> 1 tablespoon salt
> Cornmeal for dusting

Place yeast, water, and sugar in a large bowl and stir to combine. Allow to stand for about 10 minutes, until foamy.

Add chopped rosemary and 2 cups of the flour and mix well. Add the remaining flour, about 1 cup at a time. Add salt and mix. Turn dough onto a floured board and knead to form a soft, silky dough. Place in a large, greased bowl, cover, and let rise until triple in volume, 1½ to 2 hours.

Form dough into rounds or loaves. Allow to rise for about 40 minutes, or until doubled in size.

Preheat oven to 400°. Bake for 30 to 40 minutes, or until the bread is golden brown and has a hollow sound when tapped. Allow to cool for 10 minutes before slicing.

Focaccia Buns

Makes 8 buns

■ These can be used as hamburger buns, or alongside pasta or soup. You can also top the focaccia with anything from blue cheese to chopped fresh herbs.

  1 tablespoon active dry yeast
  2½ cups warm water
  2 tablespoons olive oil
  6 to 7 cups flour
  1 tablespoon salt
  ¼ cup olive oil
  2 to 3 tablespoons chopped garlic
  1 small onion, minced
  1 tablespoon cracked black pepper
  1 teaspoon kosher salt

In a large mixer bowl, combine yeast and ½ cup of water not hotter than 110°. Allow to stand for about 10 minutes, until yeast becomes foamy and creamy. Add remaining 2 cups water and the oil. Add flour, about 1 cup at a time, mixing well after each addition. Add salt and knead until dough has a smooth texture. Place dough in a lightly oiled bowl and let rise until doubled, about 1½ hours.

Shape dough into 9 by 11-inch rectangle. Cover the dough with a towel and let rise about 25 to 30 minutes. Dimple the dough with your fingertips. Cover and let rise again until doubled, about 1½ hours.

Preheat oven to 400°. Brush dough with olive oil. Then sprinkle with garlic, onion, pepper, and kosher salt. Bake for 30 to 40 minutes, or until golden brown. Remove from oven and invert so that the bottom does not get soggy. Cut into 8 squares and serve.

Cheese Scones

Makes 8 scones

■ We have used these scones in the restaurant for sandwiches, and topped them with poached eggs and hollandaise sauce. We even made tiny scones and filled them with smoked salmon for an appetizer. You can also serve them as a breakfast bread.

2¾ cups flour
1 tablespoon sugar
1 tablespoon dry mustard
2 cloves garlic, chopped
2 tablespoons baking powder
⅓ cup grated Parmesan cheese
2 teaspoons chopped thyme
1 teaspoon salt
½ cup unsalted butter
1 cup heavy cream

Preheat oven to 350°. In a medium-size mixing bowl combine flour, sugar, dry mustard, garlic, baking powder, Parmesan cheese, thyme, and salt. Cut butter into pieces. Rub butter into mixture with your fingertips, and mix in the cream until the dough just comes together.

Flour a board. Pour the dough onto the board and pat into a 1-inch-thick circle. Cut into 8 wedges. Place on a greased baking sheet and bake for 20 to 25 minutes, or until golden brown.

Bistro Challah Bread

Makes 3 loaves

■ This is the bread that we make our sandwiches with at the bistro. Once you taste this bread, there is no going back. You'll want to use it for everything from sandwiches to French toast. This is also the bread that I use for Raspberry Dessert Bruschetta.

¼ cup active dry yeast
1 cup sugar
3½ cups warm water (about 110°)
1 cup unsalted butter, melted and cooled slightly
8 eggs
10 to 12 cups flour
1 tablespoon salt

Place yeast, sugar, and warm water in a mixing bowl. Stir and let stand for about 10 minutes, until creamy and foamy. Add melted butter and eggs and mix well.

Combine flour with salt and add flour, 1 or 2 cups at a time, until mixture forms a soft dough. Pour dough out onto a well-floured board and knead until dough becomes smooth and elastic, about 5 minutes. Place dough in a large, well-greased bowl, then flip dough over to coat with oil. Cover with plastic wrap or a towel and let stand in a warm place for about 1 hour, or until doubled in size.

Preheat oven to 375°. Punch dough down and cut into 3 pieces. Form into 3 loaves and place in 3 greased loaf pans. Bake for about 1 hour, or until bread is golden brown and sounds hollow when tapped. Let cool before slicing.

■◆ Corn Muffins ◆■

Makes 1 dozen

■ These muffins are great both for breakfast and as an accompaniment to chili. They also freeze well.

> 1 cup cornmeal
> 1 cup flour
> 1 tablespoon sugar
> 1 teaspoon baking powder
> ¼ cup diced sun-dried tomatoes
> 1 tablespoon chopped fresh basil
> ½ teaspoon ground cumin
> 2 cloves garlic, chopped
> 1 fresh jalapeño, diced
> 1 cup milk
> ¼ cup vegetable oil
> 2 large eggs

Preheat oven to 350°. Place cornmeal, flour, sugar, baking powder, sun-dried tomatoes, basil, cumin, garlic, and jalapeño in a large bowl and stir together. In a small bowl, combine milk, oil, and eggs and mix well. Pour egg mixture into flour mixture and mix just until the batter comes together.

Grease a muffin tin and fill the cups about half full. Bake until golden brown, 20 to 25 minutes. Let cool 10 minutes before removing muffins from tin.

◆ Flatbread with ◆
Roasted Vegetable–Feta Spread

Serves 8

■ This is a good appetizer to serve to a large group. Accompany it with marinated goat cheese and even roasted garlic, and you have no-fuss appetizers. To save time, you can let the bread dough rise overnight in the refrigerator.

■ FLATBREAD
1¾ cups warm water (90 to 115°)
1 tablespoon sugar
1 package active dry yeast
2 tablespoons olive oil
5 to 6 cups flour
1 tablespoon salt
2 tablespoons olive oil

■ ROASTED VEGETABLE–FETA SPREAD
1 small eggplant
1 small onion, cut in half
2 tablespoons olive oil
2 red bell peppers, roasted, peeled, seeded, and chopped
   (see page 200)
¾ cup feta cheese
3 cloves garlic
2 teaspoons lemon juice
1 teaspoon cumin
Salt and black pepper to taste

For the flatbread, place water and sugar in a mixing bowl; add yeast and mix. Let stand for 10 minutes, until foamy and creamy. Add olive oil and mix. Add flour, about 1 cup at a time. When all the flour has been mixed in, add the salt and mix until you have a shaggy dough.

Place dough on a well-floured board and knead until it is smooth and elastic, about 10 minutes. Place dough in a large, greased bowl, cover, and allow to rise until doubled in size, 1 to 1½ hours.

Punch the dough down and cut it into 8 pieces. Flatten the pieces with your hand (like pizza dough) to form 4- to 5-inch circles of dough.

Heat about 1 teaspoon of the olive oil on a grill or in a sauté pan until very hot. Place one flatbread in the pan at a time and brown on each side, about 2 minutes per side. Remove from the pan and repeat with the rest of the rounds, adding more oil as necessary, until you have cooked all of the bread. When ready to serve, cut into wedges.

For the vegetable spread, preheat oven to 375°. Place eggplant and onion in a baking pan and drizzle with the olive oil. Bake until the eggplant is brown and soft to the touch, about 20 to 25 minutes. Remove from the oven and set aside until cool enough to handle.

Place peppers, feta, and garlic in a blender or food processor and process until smooth. When the eggplant is cool, cut it in half, scoop out the inside, and place in food processor. Cut the onion into large dice and place in food processor. Process until mixture is smooth. Add lemon juice, cumin, salt, and pepper and mix well. Place in a bowl and serve with wedges of flat bread.

Olive Bread

Makes 2 loaves

■ For me, making bread is a great stress reducer, and making a bread with olives in it really makes my day. Pair this bread with just about any soup or salad in the book and you have a winning meal.

    3 cups warm water (90 to 115°)
    2 tablespoons or 2 packages active dry yeast
    2 tablespoons olive oil
    1 tablespoon salt
    6 to 8 cups flour
    2 cups chopped cured olives
    2 tablespoons chopped fresh basil

Place water and yeast in a mixing bowl and stir to mix. Let stand for about 10 minutes, or until creamy and foamy. Add olive oil and salt and mix. Add flour, about 1 cup at a time, until you get a shaggy dough. Add olives and basil and mix just until olives are blended into the dough. Pour onto a floured board and knead until the dough is smooth and elastic. Place dough in a well-greased bowl and allow to rise until doubled in volume, about 1 hour.

Deflate the dough, split it into 2 pieces, and form into 2 round loaves.

Preheat oven to 400°. Let loaves rise for 20 to 25 minutes, then place on a greased baking sheet and bake for about 45 minutes, or until they are brown and sound hollow when tapped. Remove from the oven and allow to cool before slicing.

Spaghetti Squash Tossed with Roma Tomato Concassée

Serves 6

■ Spaghetti squash will take on the flavor of whatever you toss it with, and you can use it almost any way you would use noodles. This dish is infused with Italian flavors—it's like pasta with a difference. I also like it with a sweeter sauce—something with brown sugar.

> 1 large spaghetti squash, baked until fork-tender
> 5 large tomatoes, peeled and seeded
> 3 cloves garlic, chopped
> ¼ cup balsamic vinegar
> 2 tablespoons olive oil
> 1 bunch basil, julienned (about ½ cup)
> Salt to taste
> 1 tablespoon cracked black pepper
> ½ cup grated Parmesan cheese

Scrape the squash into a large bowl with a fork. Coarsely chop the tomatoes and toss with the squash.

In a small bowl, whisk together the garlic, vinegar, olive oil, and basil. Season with salt and cracked black pepper. Pour over squash and toss well. Place on a platter and sprinkle with Parmesan cheese. Serve at room temperature.

◆◆ Onion Gratin ◆◆

Serves 4

■ This dish is great for brunch or dinner. Serve with Roast Beef au Jus with Herbs and follow with Chocolate Crème Caramel for a traditional Sunday night dinner with the whole family sitting down together—always a lovely way to start the week.

> 2 tablespoons olive oil
> 4 large onions, julienned
> 2 cups heavy cream
> 4 eggs
> 3 cloves garlic, chopped
> Salt and black pepper to taste
> 1 cup bread crumbs
> ¼ cup grated Parmesan cheese

Preheat oven to 350°. Heat oil in a very large sauté pan over high heat until smoking hot. Add the onions and let brown well before stirring, 2 to 3 minutes. You want the onions to caramelize, but not burn. Allow onions to caramelize on all sides, 6 to 8 minutes total. If the onions begin to burn, reduce the heat to medium low. Place the onions in a greased casserole dish and set aside.

In a small bowl, whisk together the cream, eggs, and garlic and season with salt and pepper. Pour this mixture over the caramelized onions.

In another small bowl, mix the bread crumbs and Parmesan cheese. Spread the bread crumbs over the top of the onions. Bake for 30 to 40 minutes, or until a knife inserted in the center comes out clean. Serve hot.

◆ Grilled Corn ◆
Stuffed with Basil

Serves 6

■ Stuffing the corn under the husk adds a lot of flavor and helps to keep the corn moist while you grill it. You can use other fresh herbs such as tarragon or thyme. (Pictured opposite page 22.)

> 6 ears corn (do not remove husks)
> ¼ cup butter
> 3 cloves garlic, chopped
> 3 bunches basil, coarsely chopped (about 1 cup)
> ½ teaspoon ground cumin
> ½ teaspoon black pepper
> Pinch chile powder

Light coals or start grill. Peel back the husk of each ear of corn and remove the silk. Do not strip off the husks.

In a food processor, process the butter, garlic, basil, cumin, pepper, and chile powder until mixed well. Spread some of this mixture on each ear of corn. Bring the husks up around the corn.

Place the corn on the edge of the hottest part of the grill. Grill slowly for about 10 minutes. Be careful not to let the corn burn. Remove the husk and serve immediately.

Thyme-Marinated Grilled Asparagus

Serves 6

■ There are some vegetables that I just can't seem to get enough of when they are in season. Asparagus is one of my favorites, and this marinade is a terrific way to add flavor to this delicious vegetable.

2 pounds asparagus, tough stems trimmed
2 tablespoons red wine vinegar
2 shallots, chopped
3 cloves garlic, chopped
1 tablespoon chopped fresh thyme
1 teaspoon orange juice concentrate
1 tablespoon grain mustard
⅓ cup extra-virgin olive oil
Salt and black pepper to taste

Bring 2 quarts of salted water to a boil in a large stockpot. Add asparagus and cook until it is crisp-tender, 3 or 4 minutes, depending on the size. Drain and shock in cold ice water. Set aside.

In a bowl combine vinegar, shallots, garlic, thyme, orange juice concentrate, and mustard. Slowly whisk in the oil to blend well. Season with salt and pepper.

Pour mixture over asparagus. Let marinate while you light the coals or start the grill.

To make the grilling easier, you can place the asparagus on skewers, running a skewer through each end of the spear and fitting about 5 spears on each pair of skewers. Grill the asparagus on each side just to mark it, 1 or 2 minutes per side. Remove from the grill. Serve warm or at room temperature.

Caramelized Pearl Onions with Apple

Serves 6

■ This dish is a perfect complement to Roast Leg of Lamb. It is an easy way to dress this simple dish. Remember to let the onions caramelize: you must resist the urge to stir them too much.

> 2 tablespoons olive oil
> 2 pounds pearl onions, peeled
> ¼ cup apple cider
> ½ cup dry sherry
> 2 Granny Smith apples, cored and sliced
> Salt and black pepper to taste

Heat oil in a large sauté pan until smoking hot. Add onions and cook without stirring over low heat until they are brown and caramelized. Stir and again cook without stirring to caramelize again. Continue to cook in this manner until onions are brown and very tender. Add cider and sherry and boil to reduce until about ½ cup of liquid remains. Add sliced apples and reduce further until ¼ cup of liquid remains. Cool slightly and serve.

◆ᴬ Oven-Roasted Carrots ᴬ◆

Serves 4

■ This is a side dish that can be served with Roast Beef au Jus with Herbs or even with a simple Roast Leg of Lamb. The carrots are a bit sweet but not overly so; you can still taste the carrotty flavor.

> 1 tablespoon olive oil
> 4 medium-size carrots, sliced diagonally
> 1 tablespoon unsalted butter
> 1 tablespoon maple syrup
> Pinch ground cardamom
> Salt to taste

Preheat oven to 450°. Heat olive oil in a medium-size ovenproof sauté pan until smoking hot. Add carrots and place pan in oven. Stirring once or twice, roast until carrots are tender and brown on all sides, about 3 to 5 minutes. Remove from oven and toss with butter, maple syrup, cardamom, and salt. Serve the carrots hot.

◆◆ Sweet Potato Casserole ◆◆

Serves 6

■ This casserole is perfect for the holidays, but don't just save it for special occasions. It is a nice change of pace from the everyday potato dishes for dinner or even breakfast.

4 large sweet potatoes, peeled and thinly sliced
1 tablespoon olive oil
6 ounces pancetta, diced
1 medium onion, diced
3 cloves garlic, chopped
3 shallots, chopped
2 red bell peppers, julienned
1 cup dry sherry
Salt and black pepper to taste
½ cup grated Parmesan cheese
1 cup grated Gouda cheese

Preheat oven to 375°. Place potatoes in water to cover, and set aside. In a medium-size sauté pan, heat olive oil until hot. Add pancetta and cook until crisp and brown. Add onion, garlic, shallots, and peppers and cook until you can smell the aroma, about 2 minutes. Add sherry and boil over high heat until reduced by about half, 3 to 4 minutes. Season with salt and pepper and allow to cool.

Grease a 2-quart baking dish with a bit of olive oil or cooking spray. Line bottom of pan with a layer of potatoes. Top the first layer with one third of the onion mixture, then one third of each of the cheeses. Repeat for two more layers.

Cover with foil and bake for 30 minutes. Remove foil and cook until potatoes are fork-tender, about 15 minutes more. Remove from the oven and allow to cool for 2 minutes before cutting into pieces. Serve hot.

◆•◆ Baked Eggplant and Feta ◆•◆

Serves 6

■ This can be served as a side dish or even as a vegetarian entree. If feta is too strong for you, substitute ricotta cheese, or use half ricotta and half feta. This dish can be prepared a day ahead and then warmed in the oven before serving.

> 3 medium eggplants, sliced ½ inch thick
> ¼ cup olive oil
> 1 medium onion, julienned
> 3 cloves garlic, chopped
> 4 red bell peppers, roasted, peeled, and seeded (see page 200)
> 4 ounces feta cheese
> ½ teaspoon cracked black pepper
> 1 tablespoon chopped fresh oregano
> 1 teaspoon chopped fresh marjoram
> 1 cup fresh bread crumbs

Preheat oven to 350°. Heat 1 tablespoon of the olive oil in a large sauté pan. Add as many slices of eggplant as will fit into the pan in one layer. Brown each side well, 2 to 3 minutes per side. Remove eggplant from pan and drain on a baking sheet while you cook the rest of the eggplant, using more oil as needed. Place onions and garlic in pan and sauté until you can smell the aroma.

Lightly oil a 9-by-11-inch baking dish and layer the eggplant on the bottom of the dish. Place onion and garlic mixture and roasted red bell peppers on top of eggplant, then crumble feta on top of peppers. Sprinkle with pepper, oregano, marjoram, and bread crumbs. Bake for 20 to 25 minutes, or until golden brown. Serve warm.

Parmesan Baked Potatoes

Serves 4

■ These potatoes are so pretty—and they don't taste half-bad either. Substitute any grating cheese you like for the Parmesan cheese. You can also prepare these ahead: keep them in the refrigerator then pop them in the oven before serving.

> 4 large baking potatoes
> ½ cup half-and-half
> 2 tablespoons butter
> 3 cloves garlic, minced
> ½ cup grated Parmesan cheese
> 2 egg yolks
> 2 teaspoons chopped fresh thyme
> Salt and black pepper to taste

Preheat oven to 350°. Bake potatoes for 50 minutes to 1 hour, or until they are fork-tender. Remove from the oven and allow to cool slightly.

Cut potatoes in half and scoop the insides into a medium-size bowl. Add half-and-half and butter and mash with a potato masher. Add garlic, Parmesan cheese, egg yolks, and thyme and mix again. Season with salt and pepper.

Preheat boiler. Place potato mixture in a large piping bag fitted with a large star tip. Pipe potatoes into 8 large rosettes on a greased baking sheet. Place under broiler for about 5 minutes, or until golden brown. Serve hot.

◆ The Best Onion Rings ◆

Serves 4

■ These onion rings can go with burgers or even with barbecued chicken. Believe me, you will find things to go with these after you taste them. Try different spice mixtures, or even some dried herbs, such as basil and thyme.

> 3 medium onions, sliced ½ inch thick
> 1 cup flour
> 2 tablespoons baking powder
> 2½ tablespoons cornstarch
> About ½ cup very cold good-quality beer
> 4 cups vegetable oil, for deep-frying
> 1 tablespoon kosher salt
> ½ teaspoon cracked black pepper
> ½ teaspoon garlic powder
> Pinch ground cumin
> ½ teaspoon chile powder

Break the onion slices into rings, but do not break the rings. Mix flour, baking powder, and cornstarch in a medium-size bowl. Add enough beer to make a thick, creamy batter. Keep cold until ready to use.

Place oil in a heavy saucepan and heat to 350°. Dip onions in batter and place as many rings into the pan as will fit without crowding. Fry until golden brown. Drain on paper towels. Repeat with the rest of the onions. In a small bowl, mix salt, pepper, garlic powder, cumin, and chile powder. Season the hot onion rings with the spice mixture. Serve hot.

Vegetables Roasted in Parchment with Aged Goat Cheese

Serves 4

■ Cooking vegetables in parchment keeps them moist and flavorful, and it helps retain the vitamins in the vegetables. (Pictured opposite page 23.)

3 small carrots, diced
1 small onion, diced
2 cloves garlic, roughly chopped
1 medium-size sweet potato, diced
2 leeks, julienned
1 zucchini, diced
1 yellow squash, diced
1 teaspoon chopped fresh basil
1 teaspoon chopped fresh thyme
1 teaspoon chopped fresh savory
½ teaspoon cracked black pepper
2 teaspoons olive oil
Dash balsamic vinegar
⅓ cup grated aged goat cheese or Parmesan cheese

Preheat oven to 375°. Cut a 12-inch square of parchment paper. Fold the parchment in half-diagonally to form a triangle, then fold it back so it lays flat. In a large bowl toss together carrots, onions, garlic, sweet potato, leeks, zucchini, and yellow squash, and mix well.

Pile the vegetables in the middle of one triangle on the parchment. Sprinkle the vegetables with the basil, thyme, savory, pepper, olive oil, vinegar, and goat cheese. Fold the parchment over to form a triangle again and crimp the edges tightly. Place in a baking pan and bake for about 20 minutes. The parchment will puff up and turn golden brown. Cut the parchment open and serve the vegetables hot from the parchment.

Baked Eggplant
with Olive Stuffing

Serves 4 as an entree, 6 as a side dish

■ You can serve this as a side dish, cut into pieces, or you can serve half an eggplant as an entree, with Rosemary French Bread and a salad rounding out the meal. Peach Tart makes an appealing finish.

2 small eggplants, cut in half
2 tablespoons olive oil
1 small onion, diced
3 cloves garlic, chopped
2 medium tomatoes, seeded and diced
1 teaspoon chopped fresh marjoram
½ cup pitted chopped kalamata olives
½ cup bread crumbs
⅓ cup grated Parmesan cheese
Salt and black pepper to taste

Preheat oven to 350°. Place eggplant on a baking sheet and drizzle with 1 tablespoon of the olive oil. Bake for 20 to 30 minutes, or until tender.

While the eggplant is baking, heat the remaining 1 tablespoon olive oil in a medium sauté pan until very hot. Add onion and garlic and sauté until you can smell the aroma, 1 to 2 minutes. Add tomatoes, toss with onion, and sauté lightly. Add marjoram and sauté for about 2 minutes. Remove from heat and let cool.

Place cooled tomato mixture in a bowl and add olives, bread crumbs, and Parmesan cheese; mix well.

When eggplant is tender, remove from oven and let cool slightly. (Leave oven at 350° for baking the stuffed eggplant.) Scoop the middle of the eggplant out, leaving 1 inch of flesh all the way around. Do not break the skin. Let the eggplant flesh cool, then chop roughly and add to the stuffing. Season with salt and pepper.

Place the stuffing back into the 4 eggplant halves. Bake for 15 to 20 minutes, or until stuffing is golden brown. Serve hot.

◆▪ Orange- and Ginger- ▪◆
Scented Couscous

Serves 6

■ Couscous must be the world's easiest and most versatile side dish. It takes about ten minutes to prepare, and you can flavor it with just about anything, from fresh herbs to coconut milk. This flavor combination works well with Panfried Swordfish Steaks with Cumin.

> 3 cups Chicken or Vegetable Stock (see page 196 or page 198)
> 1 tablespoon chopped gingerroot
> 2 teaspoons orange juice concentrate
> Zest of 1 orange
> 1½ cups couscous
> ½ teaspoon unsalted butter
> Salt and black pepper to taste

Place stock, gingerroot, concentrate, and zest in a saucepan and bring to a boil. Meanwhile, place couscous in a medium-size bowl. Pour the boiling stock over the couscous and cover with plastic wrap for about 10 minutes. Remove the plastic wrap, add butter, and fluff with a fork. Season with salt and pepper, and serve.

Hazelnut Mashed Potatoes

Serves 4

■ This potato dish can be used for a side dish for just about any meal. It's great with Braised Chicken with Herbs and Shallots. If you like, you can substitute toasted pecans for the hazelnuts.

> 1 pound new potatoes, peeled and diced
> 5 cloves garlic, chopped
> ⅓ cup heavy cream
> 1 tablespoon unsalted butter
> Salt and pepper to taste
> ¼ cup toasted ground hazelnuts
> 1 teaspoon chopped fresh thyme

Place the potatoes and garlic in a medium-sized saucepan and cover with water. Over high heat, boil the potatoes until fork-tender, about 10 minutes. Strain off water and mash the potatoes with a potato masher or fork. Add cream and butter, and continue to mash by hand until smooth. Season with salt and pepper. Add hazelnuts and chopped thyme and mix well. Serve hot.

SALADS
& SOUPS

◆◆ Gorgonzola-Dressed Greens ◆◆

Serves 6

■ The dressing for this salad is similar to the one we serve on our house salad at the bistro. This salad is a wonderful addition to any meal, especially if you use greens that have different flavors and textures.

■ GORGONZOLA DRESSING
¼ cup red wine vinegar
2 shallots, chopped
3 cloves garlic, chopped
2 tablespoons Dijon-style mustard
4 ounces Gorgonzola cheese
¾ cup olive oil
Salt and black pepper to taste

■ GREENS
1 head red leaf lettuce
½ pound mesclun (mixed greens)
1 bunch radishes, sliced
2 tomatoes, cut into wedges
1 small cucumber, thinly sliced
2 ounces Gorgonzola cheese, to crumble on top

For the dressing, place vinegar, shallots, garlic, mustard, and Gorgonzola in a food processor and purée until smooth. With the motor running, slowly add the oil; process until smooth. Season with salt and pepper. Refrigerate until ready to use.

To assemble, clean lettuce and mesclun and place in a large bowl. Add radishes, tomato, and cucumber and toss. Add about ½ cup dressing and toss to coat the greens. Crumble Gorgonzola on top and serve.

Ginger, Carrot, and Daikon Salad

Serves 4

■ You can serve this salad with many different entrees—from Tuna with Five-Spice Soy Glaze to Barbecue Pork Loin with Chinese Pancakes. It's a crisp and healthful addition to any menu.

> 1 large daikon radish, julienned
> 2 medium carrots, julienned
> 6 radishes, thinly sliced
> 3 tablespoons seasoned rice vinegar
> 1 tablespoon chopped gingerroot
> 2 cloves garlic, chopped
> 1 tablespoon Asian chile sauce
> ½ teaspoon chopped cilantro
> ⅓ cup vegetable oil
> Soy sauce to taste

Place julienned daikon, carrot, and radish in a bowl and toss.

For the dressing, place vinegar, gingerroot, garlic, chile sauce, and cilantro in a small bowl and mix well. Whisk in oil until well blended. Season with soy sauce.

Pour dressing over radish mixture and marinate 30 minutes. Serve cold or at room temperature.

Wild Mushroom Salad

Serves 6

■ This salad can be used as a side dish, or as a bed for grilled beef tenderloins or rare seared tuna: the salad is so flavorful you don't even need a sauce. You can substitute it for the mushroom sauce in Beef Tenderloin with Wild Mushroom Sauce.

    1½ pounds assorted wild mushrooms
        (such as chanterelles, morels, and shiitakes)
    1 tablespoon olive oil
    3 cloves garlic, chopped
    3 shallots, chopped
    ¼ cup balsamic vinegar
    ½ cup olive oil
    1 teaspoon chopped fresh thyme
    1 teaspoon chopped fresh marjoram
    1 teaspoon chopped fresh rosemary
    1 teaspoon cracked black pepper
    Salt to taste

Slice the wild mushrooms. Heat the oil in a sauté pan until very hot. Add the mushrooms and sauté over medium heat until tender, 3 to 5 minutes. Add the shallots and garlic and sauté lightly for about 1 minute. Add vinegar and oil and bring to a boil. Add thyme, marjoram, and rosemary and simmer 2 minutes. Remove from the heat and season with pepper and salt. Cool to room temperature before serving.

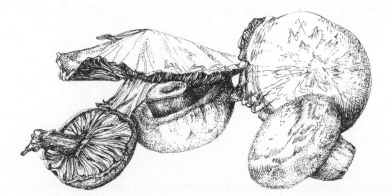

Celeriac Salad

Serves 4

■ Celeriac, also known as celery root, is really underused. The texture is better than celery but the flavor is just about the same. You can use this salad anywhere you would serve coleslaw. It's a nice change from the expected.

3 medium-size celery roots, peeled
1 small red onion, thinly sliced
3 cloves garlic, chopped
2 tablespoons Dijon-style mustard
3 tablespoons sherry vinegar
1 tablespoon fresh lemon juice
1¼ cups olive oil
1 teaspoon celery seeds
1 teaspoon chopped parsley
Salt and black pepper to taste

Grate the celery root and place in a medium-size bowl. Add red onion and toss to mix. Set aside.

Place garlic, mustard, vinegar, and lemon juice in the bowl of a food processor. With the motor running, slowly add the olive oil. Once the oil is incorporated, add the celery seed and parsley. Season with salt and pepper.

Add the dressing to the celery root mixture, and toss to mix. Chill for about 30 minutes before serving.

◼◼ Warm Spinach Salad ◼◼
with Asian Black Bean Dressing

Serves 4

◼ This is my favorite salad to make for demonstrations. People are sometimes skeptical about the black bean dressing, but when they taste it, it wins them over. You can use the leftover dressing on grilled tuna or chicken, or on blanched snowpeas or asparagus.

◼ ASIAN BLACK BEAN DRESSING

¼ cup rice vinegar
2 shallots, chopped
3 cloves garlic, chopped
1 tablespoon chopped gingerroot
2 tablespoons Dijon-style mustard
1 tablespoon orange juice concentrate
¼ cup fermented black beans, rinsed well
¾ cup vegetable oil
Pinch chile flakes
½ teaspoon soy sauce, or to taste

◼ WARM SPINACH SALAD

1 teaspoon vegetable oil
1 cup sliced wild or domestic mushrooms
1 red bell pepper, julienned
1 red onion, julienned
2 bunches spinach, stems trimmed
1 pear, cored and sliced, for garnish
Pickled ginger, for garnish

For the dressing, place vinegar, shallots, garlic, gingerroot, mustard, orange juice concentrate, and black beans in a bowl. Whisk to mix together. Slowly whisk in oil until emulsified. Season with chile flakes and soy sauce; set aside.

For the salad, heat oil in a large sauté pan until very hot. Place mushrooms in pan and sauté until tender, 2 to 3 minutes. Add pepper and onion and sauté briefly, about 1 minute. Add about ½ cup dressing to the pan and heat just until the dressing comes to a boil. While dressing is heating, place cleaned spinach in a large bowl. Pour hot dressing over spinach and toss. Place on plates or a serving platter and garnish with fresh pear slices and pickled ginger. Serve immediately.

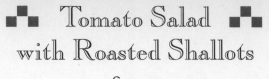

Tomato Salad with Roasted Shallots

Serves 4

■ When you are making a salad whose main ingredient is tomatoes, it is so important that you make it only when tomatoes are at their peak. Ideally, use tomatoes from your garden, or buy only vine-ripened tomatoes. Roast the shallots until they are very soft and caramelized.

> 5 large, vine-ripened tomatoes, cut into wedges
> 12 oven-roasted shallots (see page 199)
> 2 tablespoons sherry vinegar
> 3 cloves garlic, chopped
> 6 tablespoons extra-virgin olive oil
> 1 teaspoon chopped fresh thyme
> 1 teaspoon chopped fresh oregano
> 1 teaspoon cracked black pepper
> Salt to taste

Place tomato wedges in a bowl. Coarsely chop the roasted shallots and toss with the tomatoes. Place vinegar and garlic in a small bowl and whisk in olive oil to emulsify. Add thyme, oregano, and black pepper and mix well. Season with salt to taste. Pour over tomato and shallot mixture and allow to sit for 20 to 30 minutes before serving. This dish is best served at room temperature.

Caesar Salad

■ This is the traditional Caesar dressing made with coddled eggs. If you decide to use the coddled eggs, make sure that they are fresh, do not have any cracks, and have been stored properly. But if you feel unsure, leave them out—it's as simple as that. Either way, you can make the dressing up to a week ahead and store it in the refrigerator.

¾ cup grated Parmesan cheese
2 tablespoons chopped garlic
1 tablespoon Dijon-style mustard
1 anchovy fillet
3 eggs, coddled (see Glossary)
1 tablespoon cider vinegar
Juice of 2 lemons
3 dashes Tabasco sauce
3 dashes Worcestershire sauce
¾ to 1 cup olive oil
Salt and black pepper to taste
1 or 2 heads romaine lettuce
1½ cups croutons

Place ¼ cup Parmesan cheese, garlic, mustard, anchovy, eggs, vinegar, lemon juice, Tabasco sauce, and Worcestershire sauce in food processor. With the motor running, slowly add the olive oil. Season with salt and pepper and set aside.

Tear lettuce into pieces. Place in a large bowl with croutons and dressing and toss. Top with remaining Parmesan cheese.

◆■ Smoked Chicken Salad ■◆

Serves 4

■ This is a recipe that John and I created for a picnic at an herb farm. You can serve it on top of the wild greens, or you can put it between a couple of slices of good rye bread. Finish your meal with tangy Lemon Cookies.

> 1 pound smoked boneless, skinless chicken, diced (see page 195)
> ½ cup toasted chopped pecans
> 1 tablespoon olive oil
> 1 sweet onion
> 3 cloves garlic, chopped
> 3 shallots, chopped
> 2 apples, peeled, cored, and diced
> 4 stalks celery, diced
> ¼ cup apple juice
> 2 tablespoons white wine vinegar
> 1 tablespoon lemon juice
> ½ teaspoon dry mustard
> 1 tablespoon Dijon-style mustard
> 3 egg yolks
> 1 tablespoon chopped fresh marjoram
> 1½ cups olive oil
> Salt and black pepper to taste
> ½ to ¾ pound mesclun (mixed greens)
> 1 small red onion, thinly sliced
> 1 cup toasted hazelnuts or pecans

Place chicken and pecans in a large bowl. In a sauté pan, heat oil over high heat until very hot. Add sweet onion, garlic, and shallots and sauté lightly until you can smell the aroma. Add apples and celery and sauté just until the apples are crisp-tender, about 2 minutes. Add apple juice and bring to a boil. Remove from heat and allow to cool. Add to chicken and toss. Refrigerate while preparing the dressing.

For the dressing, place vinegar, lemon juice, dry mustard, Dijon-style mustard, yolks, and marjoram in a blender or food processor. With the motor running, slowly add the oil, blending until it is all incorporated. Season with salt and pepper.

Mix about 1 cup of the dressing with the cooled chicken mixture. Divide the mesclun among 4 plates, then distribute the chicken salad on top of the greens. If you like, you can drizzle the greens with any remaining dressing. Top each of the salads with thinly sliced red onion and toasted hazelnuts. Serve chilled.

◆◆ Wild Green Salad with ◆◆
Basil Dressing and Shredded Chicken

Serves 4

■ You might think the method I give for this salad a bit strange, but warming the dressing with the greens brings out the flavor. Do not overcook the greens; you want them to retain their crisp texture. (Pictured opposite page 54.)

■ BASIL DRESSING
¼ cup sherry vinegar
2 shallots, chopped
2 cloves garlic, chopped
1 tablespoon Dijon-style mustard
1 cup chopped fresh basil
¾ cup olive oil
2 teaspoons cracked black pepper
Salt to taste

■ SALAD
1 cup sliced mushrooms
4 poached or baked chicken breasts, cooled, and shredded with a fork
1½ pounds mixed wild greens
½ cup grated aged goat cheese or Parmesan cheese
1 red bell pepper, diced

For the dressing, place vinegar, shallots, garlic, mustard, and basil in a medium-size bowl and mix well. Slowly whisk in olive oil to thoroughly blend. Season with cracked black pepper and salt and mix well. Set aside in the refrigerator until ready to use.

To assemble the salad, place mushrooms, shredded chicken, greens, and about ½ cup of basil dressing in a large metal bowl. Place over high heat and toss while just warming the salad. When the greens just start to show signs of wilting, remove from the heat. Do not overcook the greens.

Divide salad among 4 plates and top with grated cheese and bell pepper. Serve immediately.

Three~Bean Salad

■ This salad is the taste of summer. It is great to bring on a picnic or to a barbecue. You can make it ahead of time, so it's perfect for warm evenings when you don't want to heat up your kitchen.

1 pound green beans, such as Blue Lake, trimmed
½ pound Romano beans, trimmed
1½ cups cooked kidney beans
Kernels cut from 3 ears corn (about 1 cup)
2 red bell peppers, diced
¼ cup cider vinegar
1 tablespoon sugar
½ cup vegetable oil
1 tablespoon fresh lemon thyme
3 cloves garlic, chopped
1 teaspoon cracked black pepper
Salt to taste

In 2 quarts of salted boiling water, blanch the green and Romano beans until crisp-tender, 2 to 3 minutes. Place in a large bowl of ice water to stop the cooking.

When beans are cool, drain and place in a large bowl. Add kidney beans, corn, and peppers and toss to mix. In a small bowl, whisk together vinegar, sugar, and vegetable oil. Pour this mixture over the beans. Add thyme, garlic, and black pepper and mix again. Season with salt and allow to marinate for at least 30 minutes. Serve chilled or at room temperature.

◆▪ Corn Salad ▪◆
with Southwestern Dressing

Serves 6

■ Make this salad in the summer when the corn is sweet: do not use frozen corn—it just isn't as good. This is a good dish to serve at a barbecue or take on a picnic.

■ SOUTHWESTERN DRESSING
2 shallots, chopped
3 cloves garlic, chopped
Juice of 1 lemon
Juice of 1 lime
1 jalapeño, diced
2 tablespoons cayenne sauce
½ cup olive oil
¼ cup sour cream
½ teaspoon chile powder
1 teaspoon ground cumin
½ teaspoon chopped cilantro
Salt and black pepper to taste

■ CORN SALAD
2 teaspoons vegetable or olive oil
Kernels cut from 6 ears of corn (about 2½ cups)
1 small red onion, diced
2 red bell peppers, roasted, peeled, seeded, and julienned (see page 200)
3 large vine-ripened tomatoes, seeded and diced
Salt and black pepper to taste

For the dressing, place shallots, garlic, lemon juice, lime juice, jalapeño, and cayenne sauce in a medium-size bowl and whisk together. Slowly whisk in oil until well blended and smooth. Add sour cream and mix again. Add chile powder, cumin, and cilantro, and season with salt and pepper. Set aside while constructing the salad.

For the salad, heat oil in a large sauté pan until very hot. Add corn and sauté for about 2 minutes. Add onion, peppers, and tomatoes and lightly sauté for another 2 minutes. Season with salt and pepper. Pour into a bowl to cool, and then toss with southwestern dressing. Serve chilled.

Seared Tuna with Greens
Tossed with Wasabi Dressing

Serves 4

■ This is an entree salad that is perfect for a summer evening. Don't overcook the tuna or it will dry out. You can make the dressing as spicy or mild as you like by adjusting wasabi.

■ WASABI DRESSING
Zest of 1 lime
Juice of 1 lime
Zest of 1 orange
Juice of 1 orange
1 tablespoon of rice vinegar
2 cloves garlic, chopped
1 tablespoon chopped gingerroot
2 tablespoons Asian chile sauce
1 tablespoon wasabi powder, mixed with 2 tablespoons hot water
¾ cup vegetable oil
Soy sauce to taste

■ SEARED TUNA WITH GREENS
¾ pound mixed wild greens
1 medium daikon radish, julienned
1 red bell pepper, julienned
6 radishes, thinly sliced
¼ pound fresh green beans, blanched
4 tuna fillets, 5 ounces each
Salt and black pepper to taste
1 tablespoon vegetable oil

For the dressing, in a medium-size bowl combine lime zest, lime juice, orange zest, orange juice, vinegar, garlic, ginger, chile sauce, and wasabi and mix well. Slowly whisk in oil until well blended. Add soy sauce to taste and set aside.

Place greens, daikon, red pepper, radishes, and green beans in a large bowl and set aside. Season tuna fillets with salt and pepper. Heat oil in a large sauté pan over high heat until smoking hot. Cook fillets for 1 to 2 minutes on each side for rare doneness. Add about ⅓ cup of the Wasabi Dressing to the greens and toss. Divide greens among 4 entree plates, then top each with a tuna fillet. Serve immediately, as tuna continues to cook from removed from pan, and you don't want it to overcook.

Crisp Sweet Potato Salad ◆ ■
with Pepper Bacon Dressing

Serves 4

■ Tired of the same old way of preparing sweet potatoes? So am I: this salad is like a twist on a warm potato salad. If you like, you can use pancetta instead of bacon in the dressing.

■ PEPPER BACON DRESSING
5 slices pepper bacon, diced
3 cloves garlic, chopped
3 shallots, chopped
2 tablespoons cider vinegar
⅓ cup olive oil
2 teaspoons chopped fresh thyme
½ teaspoon cracked black pepper
Salt to taste

■ SWEET POTATO SALAD
4 medium-size sweet potatoes, peeled, and sliced ¼ inch thick
1 tablespoon vegetable oil
1 head curly endive, separated into leaves
1 Granny Smith apple, thinly sliced
1 medium red onion, thinly sliced

For the dressing, heat a medium sauté pan, then add diced bacon and cook over high heat until the bacon starts to brown. Add garlic and shallots and cook just until you start to smell the aroma. Add vinegar and scrape the fond (browned bits) from the bottom of the pan. Add oil, thyme, and black pepper and mix. Bring to a boil, then season with salt. Set aside, keeping the dressing warm, or reheat when ready to use.

For the salad, heat olive oil in a very large sauté pan until smoking hot. Add as many slices of sweet potatoes as will fit in one layer. Do not crowd the pan. Brown the potatoes on each side, about 2 minutes per side, then drain on paper towels. Repeat with remaining potatoes. Place the endive on a large platter, or divide it among 4 individual plates. Top the endive with sweet potatoes and sliced apple. Drizzle with warm dressing and top with red onion slices. Serve warm.

Fennel Corn Chowder

Serves 6

■ This soup is a meal—lunch or dinner. Serve it with Corn Muffins or sourdough bread and everyone will be happy. I usually make this soup when corn is in season; you can use frozen corn, but don't allow it to cook too long or it will get tough.

6 slices pepper bacon, diced
1 tablespoon vegetable oil
1 yellow onion, diced
1 large fennel bulb, diced
4 cloves garlic, chopped
1 tablespoon flour
4 cups Chicken Stock (see page 196)
4 large potatoes, diced
Kernels cut from 5 ears corn (about 2 cups)
1 cup heavy cream
¼ cup cayenne sauce
Salt and black pepper to taste

In a very large stockpot, cook diced bacon until crisp. Add vegetable oil and heat. Add onion, fennel, and garlic and sauté until tender, about 2 minutes.

Add flour and stir while cooking for about 1 minute. Slowly add the chicken stock, whisking constantly to avoid lumps. Add diced potatoes and cook until barely tender.

Add corn and cream and bring to a boil. Season with cayenne sauce, salt, and pepper. Serve hot. Use less cayenne sauce if you want a less spicy soup.

Herb and Vegetable Soup

Serves 6

■ This soup is packed full of flavor and low in fat. When I make a double batch of this soup, I place the pasta in the individual serving bowls and pour the hot soup over it, so that the pasta doesn't get overcooked when I reheat the soup later.

1 tablespoon olive oil
1 large onion, diced
3 cloves garlic, chopped
1 cup sherry
3 carrots, diced
3 large potatoes, diced
2 stalks celery, diced
6 cups Chicken or Vegetable Stock
    (see page 196 or page 198)
8 coarsely chopped oven-roasted shallots
    (see page 199)
3 red bell peppers, roasted, peeled, seeded, and diced
    (see page 200)
1 tablespoon chopped fresh basil
1 tablespoon chopped fresh thyme
1 teaspoon chopped fresh rosemary
1 teaspoon chopped fresh oregano
1 teaspoon chopped parsley
2 cups cooked ziti or penne pasta
¼ cup cayenne sauce
Salt and black pepper to taste
6 herb sprigs, for garnish

In a very large stockpot, heat olive oil until very hot. Add onion and garlic and sauté until you can smell the aroma. Add sherry and boil over high heat until reduced by half, 2 to 3 minutes. Add carrots, potatoes, celery, and stock and cook over medium heat until the potatoes are barely cooked, 10 to 15 minutes. Add shallots, peppers, basil, thyme, rosemary, oregano, and parsley, and simmer just until the potatoes are fork-tender.

    Add the pasta, then season with cayenne sauce, salt, and pepper. Heat just until the pasta is warmed through. Serve soup hot, topped with a fresh herb sprig and freshly ground black pepper.

White Bean—Pancetta Soup

Serves 6

■ Beans are so versatile, plus they are good for you. We should all eat more beans and less meat, and this soup is a good place to start. Finish the meal with Cappuccino Cream Pie.

      1 tablespoon olive oil
      6 ounces pancetta, diced
      1 large onion, diced
      4 cloves garlic, chopped
      1 cup dry white wine
      1½ cups white beans, soaked overnight
      6 cups Chicken Stock (see page 196)
      2 heads garlic, roasted (see page 198)
      ¼ cup Basil Pesto (see page 205)
      Salt and black pepper to taste
      ¼ cup grated Parmesan cheese

In a large stockpot, heat olive oil until very hot. Add pancetta and cook until crisp and brown. Add onion and garlic and sauté until you can smell the aroma. Add white wine and boil until reduced by half, 3 to 5 minutes. Add beans and chicken stock and simmer over medium heat until beans are tender, about 45 minutes.

Chop the roasted garlic and add it to the soup, along with the pesto; mix well. Season with salt and pepper. Simmer the soup for another 5 to 10 minutes over low heat to develop the flavors. Serve hot topped with grated Parmesan cheese.

Spicy Beef Noodles

Serves 4

■ Once you've assembled all of the ingredients for this dish, it comes together easily. Don't be restricted by my choice of vegetables; use whatever happens to be in season. As always, you can spice this dish up or down to suit your tastes.

    1 tablespoon vegetable oil
    1 medium red onion, julienned
    4 cloves garlic, chopped
    1 tablespoon chopped gingerroot
    1 cup sliced fresh shiitake mushrooms
    2 carrots, julienned
    6 baby bok choy, cut in half, or 1 medium head bok choy, julienned
    1½ pounds sirloin, thinly sliced
    ½ pound Chinese noodles or thin-cut pasta such as spaghettini, cooked
    6 cups Beef or Chicken Stock (see page 196)
    1 tablespoon oyster sauce
    2 teaspoons Asian chile paste
    2 teaspoons dark sesame oil
    1 teaspoon orange juice concentrate
    Soy sauce to taste
    2 tablespoons toasted sesame seeds, for garnish

Heat oil in a large wok or stockpot until smoking hot. Add onion, garlic, and gingerroot and sauté until you can smell the aroma. Keep the mixture moving by stirring it so that it does not burn.

Add mushrooms and carrots and cook until carrots are crisp-tender, about 3 minutes. Add bok choy and beef and cook just until the bok choy begins to wilt, about 2 minutes.

Add noodles and stock and bring to a boil. Reduce heat to medium and simmer for 2 or 3 minutes. Add oyster sauce, chile paste, sesame oil, orange juice concentrate, and soy sauce. Simmer for 2 or 3 minutes to bring out the flavors. Serve in large bowls topped with toasted sesame seeds.

Caramelized Onion Soup

Serves 6

■ The whole key to this soup is to caramelize the onions well so that the natural sugar comes out to give this soup its sweetness. I don't suggest that you use sweet onions, such as Walla Walla onions, because they would make the soup too sweet.

2 tablespoons olive oil
4 yellow onions, julienned
2 red onions, julienned
6 shallots, chopped
6 cloves garlic, chopped
1 cup dry sherry
6 cups Chicken or Vegetable Stock
   (see page 196 or page 198)
2 cups heavy cream
1 tablespoon chopped fresh thyme
1 teaspoon crushed green peppercorns
Salt and black pepper to taste
¼ cup grated Parmesan cheese

In a large stockpot, heat oil until very hot. Add onions and shallots and cook over medium heat to caramelize them. Do not stir; allow them to brown. Watch the heat, however, so they do not burn. This process will take 15 to 20 minutes.

Add garlic and lightly sauté for 1 or 2 minutes. Add sherry and cook over low heat until reduced by about half, about 5 minutes. Add stock and reduce over high heat until about 4 cups of soup remain, 15 to 20 minutes.

Add heavy cream and cook until soup is thickened and reduced, another 5 to 10 minutes. Add thyme and green peppercorns, then season with salt and pepper. Serve hot with a bit of grated Parmesan cheese on top.

◼◾ Vegetarian Black Bean Chili ◾◼

Serves 6

◼ Like other chilis, this one is much better the next day. If I'm having guests, I make it the day before and then just heat and serve. I set up a condiment bar with salsas, sour cream, fresh avocado, and anything else that strikes my fancy. Make sure to put the beans in to soak the night before.

 2 tablespoons olive oil
 1 large onion, diced
 4 cloves garlic, diced
 2 fresh jalapeños, diced
 8 cups Vegetable Stock (see page 198)
 2 cups black beans, soaked overnight
 1 cup diced ripe tomatoes
 ½ cup diced sun-dried tomatoes
 3 red bell peppers, roasted, peeled, seeded, and diced
   (see page 200)
 3 Anaheim peppers, roasted, peeled, seeded, and diced
   (see page 200)
 2 dried ancho peppers, roasted and then pulverized
   (see page 200)
 2 teaspoons ground cumin
 1 teaspoon ground coriander
 2 teaspoons chopped fresh basil
 1 teaspoon chopped cilantro
 Salt and black pepper to taste
 1 cup salsa, as an accompaniment
 ½ cup sour cream or low-fat yogurt, as an accompaniment
 5 green onions, sliced, as an accompaniment

In a very large stockpot, heat oil until very hot. Add onion, garlic, and jalapeños and sauté lightly until you can smell the aroma. Add stock and black beans and cook over medium heat for 30 to 40 minutes, until the beans are barely tender.

Add ripe tomatoes, sun-dried tomatoes, red peppers, and Anaheim peppers and cook until the beans are tender, 15 to 20 minutes. Add ancho peppers, cumin, coriander, basil, and cilantro and allow to simmer for a few minutes. Season with salt and black pepper. Serve with salsa, sour cream, and green onions.

Smoked Tomato Soup

Serves 6

■ You will not believe the flavor that tomatoes take on when smoked. Someone once told me at the restaurant that if vegetables could always taste like this he would be a vegetarian. Smoking the tomatoes takes some time, but the soup comes together very fast after that.

    1 tablespoon olive oil
    6 slices pepper bacon, diced (optional)
    1 large onion, chopped
    1 cup red wine
    8 large tomatoes, smoked and diced (see page 201)
    4 cups Chicken or Vegetable Stock (see page 196 or page 198)
    1 teaspoon tomato paste
    2 tablespoons cayenne sauce
    1 tablespoon chopped fresh thyme
    Salt and cracked black pepper to taste

In a large stockpot, heat olive oil with bacon and cook until bacon is brown and crispy. Add onion and garlic and sauté until you can smell the aroma. Add red wine and boil over high heat until reduced by half, 3 to 4 minutes. Add tomatoes and stock and cook over medium heat until liquid has reduced by about one fourth, 10 to 15 minutes.

Add tomato paste, cayenne sauce, and thyme. Purée with a hand blender or in a food processor, then place back in pan and reheat if needed. Season with salt and pepper. Serve hot.

Scallop Seviche with Cumin Baked Tortilla Chips (page 11)

Roasted Stuffed Peppers
(page 96)

Warm Seafood Mousse with
Fennel Salsa (page 21)

Grilled Corn Stuffed with
Basil (page 37)

Vegetables Roasted in Parchment with
Aged Goat Cheese (page 45)

Sandwich with Blue Cheese, Bacon, Pears, and Arugula (page 105)

Wild Green Salad with Basil Dressing and Shredded Chicken (page 59)

Crab Relish on Risotto Cakes
(page 79)

Sautéed Fish with Tomatoes, Capers,
Asparagus, and Mustard Greens (page 86)

Polenta Sandwich with Marinated
Eggplant (page 94)

Beef Tenderloin with
Wild Mushroom Sauce (page 100)

Rack of Lamb with Hazelnut Crust
and Mustard Seed Vinaigrette
(page 114)

Chicken Consommé
with Lemon Thyme and Asparagus

Serves 4

■ Consommé is a clear soup that is fortified with meat and vegetables, which add flavor. The egg whites clear the stock and leave you with a beautiful soup. This is a very elegant way to start any meal, or you can add shredded chicken for a soup that is a light meal in itself.

½ pound ground chicken, white meat only
1 onion, finely diced
2 leeks, finely diced
2 stalks celery, finely diced
1 carrot, finely diced
1 tablespoon chopped fresh lemon thyme
½ teaspoon cracked black pepper
Zest of 1 lemon
6 egg whites, beaten until frothy
6 cups Chicken Stock (see page 196)
16 stalks asparagus, trimmed and blanched for 2 or 3 minutes
    (depending on size)
Salt and black pepper to taste

In a large bowl, combine chicken meat, onion, leeks, celery, carrot, 1½ teaspoons of the lemon thyme, pepper, and lemon zest and mix well. Add egg whites and mix well. Add vegetable mixture to cold stock and place in a large stockpot. Place on low to medium heat and bring to a boil, stirring often so that the vegetable mixture does not stick to the bottom and burn. Once the stock has come to a boil, stop stirring. The vegetable mixture will form a clump or "raft" on top of the liquid. Let the mixture boil gently for 1 hour. Don't boil it too hard or the raft will break apart.

At the end of 1 hour, turn off the stove and allow the soup to sit for 10 minutes. Strain soup through a fine strainer lined with a paper coffee filter, discarding the vegetables.

To serve, reheat soup with the remaining 1½ teaspoons of lemon thyme, and season with salt and pepper. Place 4 spears of asparagus in each serving bowl. Pour hot soup over asparagus and serve immediately.

Seafood & Vegetarian Entrees

Steamed Salmon
with Sautéed Spinach and Hazelnuts

Serves 4

■ Steaming salmon is one of my favorite methods of preparation: it keeps the salmon moist and adds lots of flavor without adding fat. When you lay it on a bed of spinach flavored with herbs and toasted hazelnuts, it's a great way to get lots of vitamins A and C.

1 lemon, cut in half
6 sprigs thyme
6 cloves garlic
4 salmon fillets, 6 ounces each
1 tablespoon olive oil
1 small onion, chopped
2 shallots, chopped
1 teaspoon chopped fresh thyme
2 teaspoons chopped fresh basil
2 tablespoons red wine vinegar
1 pound spinach, stems removed
1 teaspoon cracked black pepper
½ cup toasted, ground hazelnuts
Salt to taste

To steam the salmon, place lemon halves, thyme sprigs, and 3 of the garlic cloves in 2 cups of water in a large sauté pan. Bring to a boil. Place the salmon fillets in a large bamboo steamer, put the lid on the steamer, and place over the boiling water. Steam the salmon for 8 to 10 minutes, or until just barely done.

While the salmon is steaming, chop the remaining 3 cloves garlic, and heat the olive oil in a large sauté pan. Add onion, shallots, and chopped garlic. Sauté until you can smell the aroma. Add the thyme, basil, and vinegar. Add spinach and sauté just until it starts to wilt, 1 or 2 minutes. Do not overcook.

Remove from heat, season with pepper, and add the hazelnuts. Season with salt to taste. Place spinach on a platter and place steamed salmon on top of the spinach. Serve hot.

Penne with Smoked Salmon and Sour Cream—Chive Sauce

Serves 4

■ Penne is a tube pasta with ridges where the sauce and little bits of salmon get trapped, so it bursts with flavor when you bite into it. You can use another tube pasta or even a flat pasta, but penne is really the way to go for maximum flavor.

1 pound penne
1 tablespoon olive oil
3 cloves garlic, chopped
2 shallots, chopped
6 plum tomatoes, seeded and diced
1 cup Fish Stock (see page 197)
1 pound smoked salmon
Zest of 1 lemon
2 tablespoons lemon juice
½ cup sour cream
1 bunch chives, minced (about ¼ cup)
Salt and black pepper to taste

Cook penne until al dente and drain. Rinse. If you will be holding the penne longer than 10 to 15 minutes, toss it with a bit of olive oil to prevent sticking.

In a large sauté pan, heat olive oil until hot. Add garlic and shallots and cook until you can smell the aroma, 1 or 2 minutes. Add tomatoes and toss. Add stock and cook over medium heat until about ⅓ cup of liquid remains, 5 to 7 minutes.

Add smoked salmon and penne and toss to coat and rewarm the penne. Add lemon zest and juice and cook for about 1 minute. Add sour cream and chives and cook just until they are warmed through. Season with salt and pepper to taste. Serve hot.

Panfried Swordfish Steaks with Cumin

Serves 4

■ You can pan-fry the steaks or grill them. I serve them on a bed of Orange- and Ginger-Scented Couscous, then top with crème fraîche, and offer lime wedges on the side. Mangoes with White Chocolate Mousse is an exotic way to finish this meal.

    3 cloves garlic, crushed
    2 teaspoons minced gingerroot
    2 teaspoons ground cumin
    1 teaspoon curry powder
    Pinch chile powder
    4 swordfish steaks, 6 ounces each
    Kosher salt and black pepper to taste
    1 tablespoon vegetable oil
    ½ cup Crème Fraîche (see page 141)
    2 limes, cut in wedges

Place garlic, gingerroot, cumin, curry powder, and chile powder in a small bowl and mix well. Rub both sides of the swordfish steaks with the spice mixture. Season each side with salt and pepper to taste.

In a large sauté pan, heat the oil until smoking hot. Place steaks in pan and cook for 2 or 3 minutes on each side, until the swordfish is just cooked through. If the swordfish steaks are extra thick, you may want to finish them in the oven at 350° for 3 to 5 minutes. Remove from the pan and serve with crème fraîche and lime halves on the side.

Steamed Lingcod
with Spicy Citrus Salsa

Serves 6

■ The salsa can be made a day ahead of time if you like—it actually helps the flavors develop. If you want, you can grill the lingcod, but steaming it adds flavor and keeps it moist. This salsa works for so much more than cod: how about serving it with grilled chicken or flank steak?

■ SPICY CITRUS SALSA
2 oranges, peeled and sectioned
2 lemons, peeled and sectioned
2 limes, peeled and sectioned
1 grapefruit, peeled and sectioned
1 red onion, julienned
1 fresh jalapeño, diced
2 cloves garlic, chopped
2 teaspoons chopped gingerroot
2 tablespoons seasoned rice vinegar
3 tablespoons vegetable oil
½ teaspoon soy sauce, or to taste

■ STEAMED LINGCOD
2½ pounds lingcod fillets, cut into six 6-ounce pieces
1 lemon, cut in half
1 medium piece gingerroot, cut in half
1 stalk lemongrass, cut in half

For the salsa, place fruit sections and onion in a medium bowl. In a small bowl, whisk together jalapeño, garlic, gingerroot, and vinegar. Slowly whisk in oil. Add soy sauce. Pour over fruit sections. Allow salsa to sit at least 30 minutes before serving.

For the lingcod, place the cod in a large bamboo steamer and set aside. Combine 2 cups of water, lemon, ginger and lemongrass in a large saucepan or wok and bring to a boil over high heat. Place steamer over boiling water and cover. Steam the fish just until cooked through, 8 to 10 minutes, depending on the thickness. Remove fish from steamer and top with salsa. Serve hot.

Crab Relish on Risotto Cakes

Serves 4

■ This is a fabulous way to use leftover risotto—or any risotto you happen to over-cook. This is sort of a fusion dish: it has an Italian background and a strong Asian influence. If you like, make the relish up to a day before the cakes, then set aside in the refrigerator until you're ready to use it. (Pictured opposite page 55.)

■ CRAB RELISH
¾ pound crabmeat
1 medium cucumber, very thinly sliced
1 small red onion, sliced
2 cloves garlic, chopped
1 tablespoon chopped gingerroot
Juice of 1 lemon
Juice of 1 lime
1 tablespoon rice vinegar
2 tablespoons vegetable oil
1 teaspoon sesame oil
2 tablespoons toasted sesame seeds
Soy sauce to taste
Pinch chile flakes

■ RISOTTO CAKES
About 1½ cups leftover risotto
3 cloves garlic, chopped
2 tablespoons rice vinegar
1 teaspoon dark sesame oil
Salt and black pepper to taste
1 tablespoon vegetable oil

For the relish, place crabmeat, cucumber, red onion, garlic, and gingerroot into a medium-size bowl. Mix. Set aside. In a small bowl, combine lemon juice, lime juice, vinegar, 2 tablespoons vegetable oil, and sesame oil, and mix well. Season with sesame seed, soy sauce, and chile flakes. Toss with crab mixture. Chill in refrigerator for at least 30 minutes.

For the risotto cakes, place risotto in a large bowl. Add garlic, vinegar, and sesame oil, and mix well. Season with salt and pepper. Using about ¼ cup for each cake, form mixture into 8 cakes. Heat oil in a large pan until very hot. Cook each cake until golden brown, 2 to 3 minutes on each side. Place 2 cakes on each of 4 plates, and top with crab relish. Serve warm.

Seafood Lasagna

Serves 6

■ Even though it has some cream and cheese, boy, has this recipe been a hit! Of course you would not have this type of meal everyday: this is for a special meal or for entertaining friends. You can use all crab or all shrimp, or any other seafood you like. (In the Northwest, Dungeness is our local crab.) Fresh pasta sheets are best, but you can use the dry ones too.

■ FILLING
1 tablespoon olive oil
4 cloves garlic, chopped
3 shallots, chopped
1 medium onion, diced
1 cup dry white wine
1 pound diced white fish
8 shrimp, peeled and diced
½ cup crabmeat
Salt and black pepper to taste

■ HERB SAUCE
1 teaspoon olive oil
2 cloves garlic, chopped
3 shallots, chopped
1 small bulb fennel, diced
1 cup dry white wine
2 cups heavy cream
1 teaspoon chopped fresh basil
1 teaspoon chopped fresh thyme
1 teaspoon chopped fresh dill
Salt and black pepper to taste

■ TO ASSEMBLE
3 sheets fresh pasta (about 9 by 11 inches each)
1 cup grated Parmesan cheese

For the filling, heat oil in a large sauté pan until very hot. Add garlic, shallots, and onion and sauté until you can smell the aroma. Add white wine and boil to reduce until about ⅓ cup of wine is left. Add fish and shrimp. Cook just until the shrimp start to turn pink. Add crabmeat, toss to mix, and season with salt and pepper. Set aside in refrigerator until ready to use.

For the sauce, heat olive oil in a large saucepan until very hot. Add garlic, shallots, and fennel and sauté until you can smell the aroma. Add white wine and boil over high heat until wine is reduced by half. Add cream and, over low to medium heat, reduce the cream by half. Add basil, thyme, dill, salt, and pepper to sauce and simmer to bring out the flavors of the herbs. Let cool a bit.

To assemble the lasagna, preheat oven to 350°. Lightly grease a 9 by 11-inch baking dish. Place one sheet of pasta on the bottom of the pan. Spread about one-third of the sauce on the pasta sheet. Place about one-third of the seafood filling on top of the sauce. Top with about ⅓ cup of the Parmesan cheese. Repeat for two more layers. Bake for 25 to 30 minutes, or until golden brown. Serve hot.

◆■ Grilled Scallops ■◆
with Mango Dressing

Serves 4

■ Grilling scallops can be a bit difficult because they are very moist. Make sure that you use a very clean and well oiled grill so the scallops don't stick. As the name suggests, the mango sauce can also be used as a dressing for salad.

■ MANGO DRESSING
2 very ripe mangoes, peeled and diced
1 tablespoon chopped gingerroot
2 cloves garlic, chopped
¼ cup rice vinegar
¼ tablespoon vegetable oil
¼ cup Asian chile sauce
Salt and black pepper to taste

■ GRILLED SCALLOPS
1½ pounds large sea scallops
2 teaspoons vegetable oil
Salt and black pepper to taste

For the dressing, place mango, gingerroot, garlic, and vinegar in a blender. Purée. Add oil and chile sauce and blend to mix. Season with salt and pepper. Set aside.

For the scallops, light coals or start grill. Toss scallops with oil and season with salt and pepper. You may skewer the scallops if you like. Grill scallops 1 or 2 minutes per side, depending on the size. Divide the scallops among 4 plates and serve with mango dressing.

Tuna with Five-Spice Soy Glaze

Serves 4

■ I cannot stress enough that you should not overcook the tuna, or it will become very dry. Also, since the tuna will be rare, be sure to purchase the best-quality tuna you can.

■ SOY GLAZE
2 teaspoons vegetable oil
2 cloves garlic, chopped
2 shallots, chopped
2 teaspoons chopped gingerroot
¼ cup sherry
2 tablespoons honey
½ cup Fish or Chicken Stock (see page 197 or page 196)
¼ cup soy sauce
½ teaspoon Asian chile sauce
2 teaspoons five-spice powder
Pinch black pepper

■ TO ASSEMBLE
4 ahi tuna steaks, 6 ounces each
1 tablespoon vegetable oil

For the glaze, in a medium sauté pan, heat oil until very hot. Add garlic, shallots, and gingerroot. Sauté until you can smell the aroma. Add sherry and bring to a boil. Add honey and chicken stock, bring to a boil, and reduce slightly. Add soy sauce, chile sauce, five-spice powder, and black pepper. Set aside to cool.

To assemble the dish, place tuna steaks in soy glaze. Heat oil in a very large sauté pan until smoking hot. Remove steaks from glaze and place in pan. Cook for 2 to 3 minutes per side, depending on the thickness of the steaks. Tuna should be served rare. The more it cooks, the drier it will become. You may baste the tuna with the glaze as it cooks. Serve immediately.

Panfried Fish Sandwiches
with Spicy Tartar Sauce

Serves 4

■ This is a new twist on an old favorite. I like to pair this dish with Celeriac Salad as a side dish. To finish the meal, try Peach Gratin.

■ SPICY TARTAR SAUCE
3 cloves garlic, chopped
2 shallots, chopped
3 egg yolks
1 tablespoon Dijon-style mustard
2 tablespoons lemon juice
¼ cup white wine vinegar
1½ cups olive oil
1 tablespoon capers
2 tablespoons chopped gherkins
2 teaspoons chopped fresh tarragon
1 tablespoon Asian chile paste
Salt and black pepper to taste

■ PANFRIED FISH SANDWICHES
4 halibut fillets (or other mild white fish), 6 ounces each
Salt and black pepper to taste
½ cup flour
1 teaspoon chile powder
½ teaspoon dried thyme
½ teaspoon dried basil
1 tablespoon olive oil
4 good-quality French rolls
4 large leaves lettuce
4 thin slices red onion

For the tartar sauce, place garlic, shallots, egg yolks, mustard, lemon juice, and vinegar in a food processor and process to mix well. With the machine running, slowly add the oil. Process until all the oil is incorporated. Place in a medium-size bowl and add capers, gherkins, tarragon, and chile paste; mix well. Season with salt and pepper. Refrigerate until ready to use.

For the sandwiches, season the fillets with salt and pepper. In a small bowl, mix flour, chile powder, thyme, and basil. Dredge the fillets in the flour to coat them.

In a large sauté pan, heat olive oil until very hot. Add the fillets and brown well on each side over high heat, 2 to 3 minutes per side. If the fillets are thick, you may need to place them in a 350° oven for 3 to 4 minutes to cook them through.

Toast rolls while fish is cooking. Place fillets on toasted rolls and top with tartar sauce. Then top with lettuce and sliced onion. Serve hot.

Sautéed Fish with Tomatoes, Capers, Asparagus, and Mustard Greens

Serves 4

■ This is a one-pan meal. You sauté the fish and make the sauce in the same pan. When you do this you get so much more flavor from your sauce because of the fond—material that sticks to the bottom of the pan. Finish this light meal with a decadent Chocolate Crème Caramel. (Pictured opposite.)

4 white fish fillets, such as lingcod, 6 ounces each

Salt and black pepper to taste

½ cup flour

1 tablespoon olive oil

2 cloves garlic, chopped

¾ cup white wine

½ cup Fish Stock (see page 197)

2 teaspoons capers

Juice of 1 lemon

2 vine-ripened tomatoes, seeded and chopped

6 stalks asparagus, sliced on the diagonal

1 bunch (about 2 cups) mustard greens, julienned

3 tablespoons unsalted butter

2 teaspoons fresh tarragon

Preheat oven to 350°. Season fish with salt and pepper, then dredge in the flour to coat. Heat olive oil in a large ovenproof sauté pan until very hot. Add fish and brown well on each side, about 2 minutes per side. Bake in oven for 5 or 6 minutes more, or until the fish is just cooked through. Remove from oven and place fish on a tray.

Place the sauté pan on high heat, add garlic and white wine, and cook, scraping the bottom of the pan to remove the fond. Add the fish stock and boil to reduce a bit, 2 to 3 minutes. Add capers, lemon juice, tomatoes, and asparagus and cook over high heat just until the asparagus is tender, 2 to 3 minutes. Add mustard greens and cook just until they begin to wilt. Stir in butter, then tarragon, and season with salt and pepper. Pour mixture over fish and serve hot.

Oven-Baked Seafood Stew

■ This seafood stew is very inviting; it will make your whole house smell wonderful. It's simple to prepare because it is baked in the oven instead of for hours on top of the stove. Serve it with large pieces of warm crusty French bread.

1 small onion, julienned
1 small fennel bulb, julienned
3 cloves garlic, chopped
4 lingcod fillets (or other mild white fish), 6 ounces each
1 pound mussels, scrubbed and debearded (see Glossary)
8 extra-large shrimp, peeled and deveined
½ cup pitted, chopped kalamata olives
¼ cup pitted, chopped cured green olives
4 plum tomatoes, seeded and chopped
2 teaspoons chopped fresh thyme
2 teaspoons chopped fresh marjoram
2 tablespoons cayenne sauce
1 cup dry red wine
⅓ cup olive oil
Salt and black pepper to taste
⅓ cup grated Parmesan cheese

Preheat oven to 350°. Cover the bottom of a large casserole dish with the julienned onion and fennel root. Sprinkle with garlic, then lay fish on top of onion mixture. Lay the rest of the seafood on the bed of onions. Add olives, tomatoes, thyme, and marjoram. Drizzle with cayenne sauce, red wine, and olive oil. Season with salt and pepper.

Cover and bake for 30 to 45 minutes, or until the mussels open and the shrimp are pink. Top with Parmesan cheese and serve hot with grilled French bread.

Vegetable Cannelloni
with Sherry Sauce

Serves 4

■ You can prepare this the night before, store in the pan in the refrigerator, then bring the pan up to room temperature and place in the oven. Serve it with Gorgonzola-Dressed Greens and good French bread. Even kids like this vegetarian dish.

■ SHERRY SAUCE
1 teaspoon olive oil
2 cloves garlic, chopped
2 shallots, chopped
1 cup dry sherry
2 cups heavy cream
Salt to taste
½ teaspoon cracked black pepper

■ VEGETABLE CANNELLONI
1 tablespoon olive oil
3 cloves garlic, chopped
3 shallots, chopped
1 medium onion, diced
1 cup sliced mushrooms
1 zucchini, finely diced
1 eggplant, finely diced
2 red bell peppers, roasted, peeled, and diced (see page 200)
1 teaspoon chopped fresh oregano
1 teaspoon chopped fresh basil
¾ cup ricotta cheese
1 cup grated Parmesan cheese
Salt and black pepper to taste
8 cannelloni shells, cooked al dente

To make the sherry sauce, heat olive oil in a saucepan until very hot. Add garlic and shallots and sauté lightly. Add sherry and boil over high heat to reduce until about ⅓ cup remains. Add cream and boil over high heat until about 1 cup of liquid remains. Season with salt and pepper, and set aside.

Preheat oven to 350°. Heat olive oil in a very large sauté pan until very hot. Add garlic, shallots, and onion and sauté until you can smell the aroma, about 2 minutes. Add mushrooms, zucchini, and eggplant and cook until crisp-tender. Add peppers, oregano, and basil and sauté for 2 to 3 minutes. Remove from the heat and allow to cool.

In a medium-size mixing bowl, combine ricotta cheese and ½ cup of the Parmesan cheese. Add cooked vegetable mixture. Mix well and season with salt and pepper.

With either a spoon or a pastry bag, fill the cannelloni shells well. Place in a lightly oiled 9 by 11-inch baking dish. Top with Sherry Sauce and the remaining ½ cup Parmesan cheese. Bake for 25 to 30 minutes, or until cheese is golden brown.

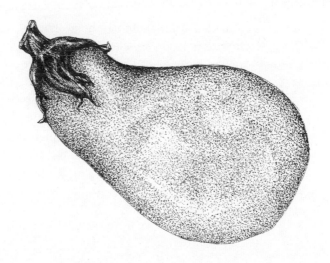

Oven-Poached Halibut
with Almond Sauce

Serves 4

■ Oven poaching is a great way to cook halibut; it's easy and keeps the fish moist. Serve this in a soup plate so you don't lose a drop of the sauce.

■ ALMOND SAUCE
2 teaspoons olive oil
3 cloves garlic, chopped
2 shallots, chopped
1 cup white wine
1½ cups Fish Stock (see page 197)
½ cup toasted, ground almonds
2 tablespoons lemon juice
1 teaspoon chopped fresh thyme
Salt and black pepper to taste

■ POACHED HALIBUT
1 tablespoon unsalted butter
4 halibut fillets, 6 ounces each
⅓ cup dry white wine
Salt and black pepper to taste

For the almond sauce, in a medium-size sauté pan heat olive oil until very hot. Add garlic and shallots and sauté until you can smell the aroma, about 1 minute. Add wine and boil over high heat to reduce until about ¼ cup of liquid remains, about 3 minutes. Add fish stock and reduce again until liquid is reduced to about 1 cup, another 3 to 4 minutes. Add nuts, lemon juice, and thyme and mix well. Season with salt and pepper and keep warm while you prepare the halibut.

For the fish, preheat oven to 350°. Butter a baking pan, then lay the fillets in the pan. Drizzle with white wine and season with salt and pepper.

Bake for 8 to 10 minutes, or until the halibut is just cooked through. Remove from oven and place a piece of halibut in each soup plate. Spoon the Almond Sauce over the fillets and serve hot.

◆◆ Roasted Shallot Risotto ◆◆

Serves 4

■ Risotto is a very popular dish, but people are often afraid to prepare it at home because it has the mystique of being very difficult to master. As long as you follow a few simple steps (toasting the rice, keeping the stock hot, and stirring), you can master the technique and create all types of exciting risotto dishes.

> 1 tablespoon butter
> 1 small onion, diced
> 2 cloves garlic, chopped
> 5 oven-roasted shallots (see page 199)
> 2 cups arborio rice
> 6 cups Chicken or Vegetable Stock (see page 196 or page 197)
>   simmering hot
> 1 tablespoon chopped fresh thyme
> ⅔ cup grated Parmesan cheese
> Salt and cracked black pepper to taste

In a large stockpot, heat butter until very hot. Add onion and garlic and sauté until you can smell the aroma. Coarsely chop the roasted shallots and add to pan. Add rice and mix well to coat the grains. Sauté the rice for a few moments.

Add about 2 cups of the stock and stir over medium heat. Stir often while the rice is cooking. Once the stock has been absorbed, add more stock and continue the process until the rice is cooked al dente. Add thyme and about ⅓ cup of the Parmesan cheese; season with salt and black pepper. Top each plate of risotto with some of the remaining Parmesan cheese.

Pepper, Olive, and Feta Pizza

Serves 1 or 2

■ Getting everyone together in the kitchen to make pizza can be lots of fun. You can make a double batch of the dough and freeze half, then pull it out the day before you want to use it and let it thaw in the refrigerator overnight.

■ PIZZA DOUGH
1 tablespoon active dry yeast
1¼ cups warm water (about 110°)
½ teaspoon sugar
2 tablespoons olive oil
3 cloves garlic, chopped
1 tablespoon chopped fresh basil
1 teaspoon cracked black pepper
3 cups flour
1 teaspoon salt

■ PIZZA TOPPINGS
½ cup cured black olives
½ cup cured green olives
3 cloves garlic, chopped
1 teaspoon capers
1 anchovy fillet
1 teaspoon lemon juice
3 tablespoons olive oil
3 red bell peppers, roasted, peeled, seeded,
    and julienned (see page 200)
1 cup feta cheese, crumbled

For the dough, place yeast, ¼ cup of the warm water, and sugar in a mixing bowl. Stir and let stand for about 10 minutes, or until creamy and foamy.

Add remaining 1 cup water, olive oil, garlic, basil, and pepper and stir. Using the dough hook of an electric mixter, mix in flour, about 1 cup at a time. Add salt and mix until a soft dough forms.

Place dough on a well-floured surface and knead to form a smooth, elastic dough, 3 to 4 minutes. Place dough in a large, greased bowl, cover, and let rise until doubled in size, about 1½ hours.

Meanwhile, prepare the olive tapenade. Place olives, garlic, capers, and anchovy in a food processor and purée until mixture forms a paste. Stop the machine, add lemon juice, olive oil, and 1 cup of water, and process until incorporated. Remove mixture from machine and set aside until ready to use.

When dough has doubled, punch down and turn out onto a well-floured board. Roll out or stretch to a 12-inch circle about ¼ inch thick.

Preheat oven to 450°. Grease a baking sheet and dust with cornmeal. Place dough in pan. Spread with the olive tapenade, then sprinkle with the peppers and crumbled feta. Bake until golden brown, 15 to 20 minutes. Allow pizza to rest a minute before slicing.

Polenta Sandwich
with Marinated Eggplant

Serves 4

■ When we had this dish on the menu at the restaurant, we would have all the components ready and then bake them to order. You can do the same; it makes life a lot easier. If you want a sauce with this dish, try Roasted Red Pepper Sauce or a simple tomato sauce. (Pictured opposite page 87.)

■ POLENTA
2 cups Vegetable Stock (see page 198)
1 tablespoon chopped fresh basil
2 cloves garlic, chopped
1 cup finely ground cornmeal
¼ cup soft goat cheese
1 teaspoon unsalted butter
Salt and black pepper to taste

■ MARINATED EGGPLANT
1 small to medium eggplant, cut into 8 slices
2 cloves garlic, chopped
2 tablespoons balsamic vinegar
¼ cup plus 2 tablespoons olive oil
½ teaspoon cracked black pepper
½ teaspoon chopped fresh thyme

■ TO ASSEMBLE
⅓ cup soft goat cheese
8 slices mozzarella cheese

For the polenta, place stock, basil, and garlic in a medium-size saucepan and bring to a boil. Slowly whisk in cornmeal, so that you don't get lumps. Cook over medium heat, stirring, until mixture thickens, 4 to 5 minutes. Remove from heat and stir in goat cheese and butter, mixing well. Season with salt and pepper.

Grease an 8 by 8-inch pan, pour polenta into pan, and spread evenly. Chill until polenta is set, about 1 hour. In the meantime, prepare the eggplant.

Place the eggplant in a large bowl. In a small bowl stir together garlic, vinegar, ¼ cup oil, pepper, and thyme, mixing well. Pour marinade over eggplant and marinate for at least 1 hour.

Heat 2 tablespoons oil in a large sauté pan until very hot. Add as many slices of eggplant as will fit in the pan, and brown on both sides, about 3 minutes per side. Remove from the pan and drain on a plate. Set aside.

To assemble, preheat oven to 350°. Remove polenta from pan and cut into 8 equal squares. Place 4 polenta squares in a greased baking pan and spread each square with about 2 teaspoons of goat cheese. Place a slice of cooked eggplant on top of each square. Then top with a slice of mozzarella and another square of polenta. Place 2 more teaspoons of goat cheese on top of the polenta, then add a second slice of eggplant and mozzarella. Bake for about 20 minutes, or until mozzarella is melted and starting to turn brown. Remove from oven and serve hot with tomato sauce or Roasted Pepper Salsa (page 200).

Roasted Stuffed Peppers

Serves 4

■ I remember stuffed peppers from childhood—I loved the stuffing but I never wanted to eat the pepper. It was kind of bitter and not very appealing. So I thought, what about sweet roasted peppers stuffed with a curry rice filling? You won't pass up a single bite of this dish. (Pictured opposite page 7.)

2 teaspoons olive oil
3 cloves garlic, chopped
1 small onion, diced
2 teaspoons chopped gingerroot
2 cups cooked rice
⅓ cup diced fresh mozzarella
¼ cup heavy cream
2 teaspoons curry powder
Salt and cracked black pepper to taste
4 whole red or yellow bell peppers, roasted (see page 200)

Heat olive oil in a sauté pan until very hot. Add garlic, onion, and gingerroot and sauté until you can smell the aroma. Add rice and toss. Remove from the heat. Add mozzarella, cream, curry powder, salt, and pepper. Mix well and cool before stuffing the peppers.

Preheat oven to 375°. Peel peppers carefully to keep them whole. Cut off the tops and remove the seeds. Stuff each of the peppers with about ½ cup of stuffing. Place on a baking sheet greased with olive oil. Bake for 20 to 25 minutes. Serve hot.

MEAT & POULTRY ENTREES

◆■ New York Steaks ■◆
with Black Bean Relish

Serves 4

■ You could begin this meal with Scallop Seviche with Cumin Baked Tortilla Chips. If you like, you can add sautéed seasonal vegetables (like squash or fresh green beans) to the black bean relish, so you have your starch and vegetable combined, then serve the steaks on a bed of relish.

■ BLACK BEAN RELISH
1 ½ cups cooked black beans
2 teaspoons vegetable oil
1 red onion, diced
3 cloves garlic, chopped
2 fresh jalapeños, diced
2 red bell peppers, roasted, peeled and diced (see page 200)
¼ cup balsamic vinegar
½ teaspoon chopped cilantro
1 teaspoon chopped fresh basil
1 teaspoon ground cumin
Salt and black pepper to taste

■ STEAKS
1 tablespoon olive oil
4 New York steaks, 6 ounces each
Salt and black pepper to taste

For the relish, place cooked black beans in a large bowl. In a large sauté pan, heat vegetable oil until very hot. Add red onion, garlic, and diced jalapeños and sauté over high heat until you can smell the aroma, 1 or 2 minutes. Add the roasted red peppers and vinegar. Bring to a boil and add cilantro and basil. Season with cumin and salt and pepper. Pour over beans and toss well. Let cool to room temperature.

For the steaks, preheat oven to 350°. In a large, ovenproof sauté pan, heat olive oil until smoking hot. Season the steaks with salt and pepper. Put the steaks in the pan and sear both sides well, 2 or 3 minutes per side. Place in oven and cook 4 to 5 minutes more, until steaks are medium rare. Remove from the oven and place each steak on a bed of black bean relish. Serve hot.

◆◆ Beef Tenderloin ◆◆
with Wild Mushroom Sauce

Serves 4

■ With this sauce, use the best mushrooms you can find. If you can't find fresh wild mushrooms in your area, try fresh domestic mushrooms and a few dried wild mushrooms. Rehydrate the dried mushrooms in either hot water or heated wine, allowing them to sit until they are soft. Add the liquid to the sauce. You can use this sauce on other cuts of meat, such as grilled tuna. (Pictured opposite page 102.)

■ WILD MUSHROOM SAUCE
½ pound wild mushrooms (such as chanterelles or morels)
1 tablespoon olive oil
2 shallots, chopped
3 cloves garlic, chopped
½ cup red wine
1 cup rich Beef Stock (see page 196)
1 teaspoon chopped fresh rosemary
¼ cup heavy cream
Salt and black pepper to taste

■ BEEF TENDERLOINS
1 tablespoon olive oil
4 beef tenderloins, 5 to 6 ounces each
1 tablespoon cracked black pepper
Salt to taste
4 ounces Gorgonzola cheese

For the sauce, slice mushrooms and set aside. In a large sauté pan, heat the oil until very hot. Add mushrooms and sauté until tender, 3 to 4 minutes. Add shallots and garlic and sauté lightly. Add wine and boil over medium heat until reduced by half, about 2 minutes. Add stock and reduce by half again, 4 to 5 minutes. Add rosemary and cream and cook for 2 to 3 minutes to reduce slightly. Season with salt and pepper. Keep sauce warm while cooking the tenderloins.

For the tenderloins, preheat oven to 350°. Heat oil in a large sauté pan until smoking hot. While the oil is heating, coat the tenderloins with pepper and season with salt. Sear each side in the hot pan until brown, 2 to 3 minutes total. Place in oven for about 4 minutes more, until tenderloins are medium-rare.

Place tenderloins on plates or a platter and spoon the mushroom sauce over them. Crumble the Gorgonzola cheese over the top and serve hot.

◆▪ Grilled Flank Steak ▪◆
with Hot Pepper Paste

Serves 4

▪ Here flank steak is marinated in a sweet and spicy marinade that flavors and tenderizes the meat. Remember, the longer you cook flank steak, the tougher it gets; I suggest not cooking it past the medium-rare stage. If you think the paste might be too spicy for someone, serve it on the side and let your guests decide how much they would like.

▪ GRILLED FLANK STEAK
2 pounds flank steak
2 tablespoons honey
2 tablespoons soy sauce
2 tablespoons rice vinegar
½ teaspoon Sichuan peppercorns

▪ HOT PEPPER PASTE
6 jalapeños, roasted and peeled (see page 200)
2 ancho peppers, roasted and peeled (see page 200)
1 red bell pepper, roasted and peeled (see page 200)
2 cloves garlic, chopped
1 teaspoon chopped parsley
1 teaspoon ground cumin
1 teaspoon balsamic vinegar
¼ cup olive oil
Salt and black pepper to taste

For the steak, place the flank steak in a baking pan. In a small bowl, mix together honey, soy sauce, vinegar, and peppercorns. Rub this mixture all over the flank steak and refrigerate for 2 to 24 hours.

For the pepper paste, place peppers in a food processor and process to chop the peppers. Add garlic, parsley, cumin, vinegar, and oil, and process until smooth. Season with salt and black pepper. Remove from the processor and refrigerate until ready to use.

To cook the steak, oil the grill rack, then light coals or start grill. Heat just until you can hold your hand over the grill for no more than 5 seconds. Grill the flank steak for 3 to 4 minutes on each side, depending on the thickness, for rare to medium-rare doneness. Remove from the heat, allow to stand for 1 or 2 minutes, then slice thinly on an angle. Serve hot pepper paste on the side or on top of the sliced steak.

Roast Beef au Jus
with Herbs

Serves 4

■ I wanted to include this simple recipe to really demonstrate how to cook a roast. Since I want to talk more about technique, I have kept the recipe simple; use your imagination to embellish this recipe.

2- to 2½-pound beef roast
1 tablespoon cracked black pepper
Salt to taste
1 bunch whole thyme sprigs
1 bunch whole sage sprigs
1 tablespoon olive oil
½ cup red wine
2 cups Beef or Chicken Stock (see page 196)
1 teaspoon chopped fresh thyme
1 teaspoon chopped fresh marjoram

Preheat oven to 350°. Season roast with cracked pepper and salt. Lay sprigs of thyme and sage on top of the roast and tie with butcher's twine. Heat oil in a roasting pan on the stovetop until smoking hot. Place roast in pan and sear well on all sides. Roast in oven for about 20 minutes for medium-rare doneness. Remove roast and allow to rest while finishing the sauce.

Place roasting pan on burner over high heat. Add wine and scrape the pan to remove the browned bits from the bottom. Boil until the wine is reduced by half. Add stock and reduce again until about 1½ cups of liquid remain. Add thyme and marjoram and season sauce with salt and pepper if needed. Slice roast and serve sauce on the side.

Osso Buco
with Lemon and Olives

Serves 4

■ This is a very Mediterranean-inspired dish with lemon and cured olives. Your house will smell good while you are cooking this dish, and when it's done you will have a tender, flavorful dish perfect for a cozy evening at home. Serve over a bed of couscous or rice.

4 veal shanks, 10 ounces each
½ cup flour
1 tablespoon olive oil
2 shallots, chopped
4 cloves garlic, chopped
½ cup dry white wine
Zest of 1 lemon
Juice of 1 lemon
½ cup pitted, chopped kalamata olives
2 cups Veal or Chicken Stock (see page 196)
1 tablespoon chopped fresh basil
½ teaspoon chopped fresh rosemary
Salt and black pepper to taste

Preheat oven to 350°. Dust veal shanks with flour. Heat a large, flameproof baking dish with olive oil until smoking hot. Add veal shanks and brown well on each side, about 2 minutes per side. Add shallots and garlic and sauté lightly for about 1 minute. Add white wine and boil until reduced by half, 3 to 4 minutes. Add lemon zest, juice, olives, and stock.

Cover with a lid or foil and bake for about 30 minutes. Add basil and rosemary, cover, and bake for 30 to 40 minutes more, until shankes are tender. Season with salt and pepper. Serve hot over couscous or rice.

Salt and Pepper–Encrusted
Roast Beef Sandwich au Jus with Chipotle

Serves 6

■ This is my version of a French Dip. Chipotles are smoked, dried jalapeños: they add a smoky, rich, and spicy flavor to soups and sauces.

2½-pound top round or bottom round beef roast
2 tablespoons cracked black pepper
2 teaspoons kosher salt
1 tablespoon olive oil
1 cup dry red wine
2 shallots, chopped
2 cloves garlic, chopped
2 cups Beef Stock (see page 196)
2 chipotle peppers
1 teaspoon chopped fresh thyme
Salt and black pepper to taste

■ TO ASSEMBLE
6 French rolls, toasted

For the roast, preheat oven to 350°. Rub the pepper and kosher salt into the beef, then set aside. Heat olive oil in a large, ovenproof sauté pan until smoking hot. Add roast and sear well on all sides, about 5 minutes total. Place in oven and roast for about 20 minutes for medium-rare to medium doneness (internal temperature of roast should be 135–140°). Let rest for 2 minutes before slicing the roast.

While the roast is cooking, make the sauce. Place red wine, shallots, and garlic in a medium-size pan and boil over high heat until the wine is reduced to about ⅓ cup, 4 to 5 minutes. Add stock, peppers, and thyme and cook over low to medium heat until reduced to about 2 cups, about 10 minutes. Season with salt and pepper and keep warm.

To assemble the sandwich, slice the beef and place on toasted French rolls. Serve the sauce on the side in a container that is wide enough to dip the sandwich in. Serve warm.

Sandwiches with Blue Cheese, Bacon, Pears, and Arugula

Makes 6 sandwiches

■ I like to pack these sandwiches when we go on wine-tasting picnics in the Oregon wine country. I never forget to pack White Chocolate–Hazelnut Macaroons—hazelnuts are grown in the wine country, too. The sandwiches, macaroons, and wine complement each other perfectly. (Pictured opposite page 54.)

½ cup good-quality blue cheese
3 tablespoons heavy cream
2 cloves garlic, chopped
12 slices good-quality bread or Bistro Challah (see page 30)
1 large or 2 medium pears, sliced (about 18 thin slices)
12 slices pepper bacon, cooked until crisp
½ pound arugula, cleaned

Combine blue cheese, cream, and garlic in a small bowl. Spread this mixture on 6 of the slices of bread. Place 3 pear slices on each of the 6 bread slices. Then top each slice with 2 slices of bacon. Distribute the arugula among the 6 sandwiches. Top with the remaining 6 slices of bread and serve.

Pork Tenderloins
with Dried Cherry Sauce

Serves 4

■ Tenderloin is one of my favorite cuts of pork. It cooks quickly, and it's tender and lower in fat than beef tenderloin. Just make sure that you do not overcook it—because it is so low in fat, it will dry out. This dried cherry sauce is also low in fat but the cherries give it a rich flavor.

■ DRIED CHERRY SAUCE
1 cup dry red wine
2 shallots, chopped
3 cloves garlic, chopped
1 cup dried cherries
1 tablespoon chopped gingerroot
2 cups rich Chicken Stock (see page 196)
2 tablespoons unsalted butter
1 teaspoon cracked black pepper
Salt to taste

■ PORK TENDERLOINS
4 pieces of pork tenderloin, 6 ounces each
1 teaspoon curry powder
Salt and black pepper to taste
1 tablespoon vegetable oil

For the sauce, place wine, shallots, garlic, cherries, and gingerroot in a large saucepan. Over high heat, boil to reduce the mixture until about ¼ cup of wine remains, 4 to 5 minutes. Add chicken stock and boil over high heat until reduced by half, about 5 minutes.

Purée the reduced mixture in a blender or food processor until smooth. Return it to the saucepan and, over medium heat, whisk in butter and season with pepper and salt. Keep sauce warm while preparing the tenderloins.

To prepare the tenderloins, preheat the oven to 350°. Season the tenderloins with curry powder, salt, and pepper. Set aside. Heat oil in a large, ovenproof sauté pan until smoking hot. Add pork and sear on both sides, about 2 to 3 minutes total. Place pan in oven for 5 to 8 minutes for medium doneness, depending on the thickness of the tenderloin. Remove from oven and allow to rest for a minute. Slice the pork and dividing among 4 plates. Serve hot with the Dried Cherry Sauce.

Barbecue Pork Loin
with Chinese Pancakes

Serves 4

■ This dish can be served as an entree or an appetizer. The pancakes are great—you can stuff them with all kinds of things: fresh crab and sautéed shrimp are especially good. On the side you can serve Chinese mustard and toasted sesame seeds.

■ BARBECUE PORK LOIN
3 cloves garlic, chopped
1 tablespoon chopped gingerroot
1 cup hoisin sauce
2 teaspoons chile flakes
2 pounds boneless pork loin, fat trimmed

■ CHINESE PANCAKES
2 cups flour
¾ cup boiling water
⅓ cup light sesame oil
Vegetable oil for frying

For the pork loin, in a medium-size bowl, mix together garlic, gingerroot, hoisin sauce, and chile flakes. Rub this mixture over the pork loin and allow it to marinate for at least 4 hours; overnight is better.

Preheat oven to 375°. Remove excess sauce from pork. Coat pork with sesame seeds. Place in a roasting pan. Roast for 30 to 40 minutes for medium-well doneness. Allow to rest for a minute or two before slicing.

For the pancakes, place flour in a medium bowl, add water, and stir to form a soft dough. Allow to rest for 15 minutes.

Roll dough out on floured board. With a small (½-inch) round cookie cutter, cut circles. Make an even number of circles; you should have 8 to 12. Lightly flour a clean board. Place one circle of dough on the board; place a drop of sesame oil in the middle. Place another circle on top of the first. Roll the circles out, making each into one very thin circle. It should be 3 times the size of the original circle.

Heat a nonstick pan until hot. Place a bit of vegetable oil in the pan. Fry the pancakes for about 1 minute on each side, or until lightly browned. When the pancakes are cooked on both sides, remove from the heat and pull the two pancakes apart. Cover pancakes with a cloth to keep warm if serving right away. Serve with barbecue pork loin. The pork is rolled up in each pancake, burrito style.

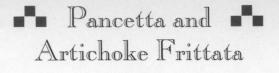

Pancetta and Artichoke Frittata

Serves 6

■ I like to make frittatas when I am feeding more than two people—they are so easy to cut and serve. Frittatas are also a great way to use leftovers.

4 ounces pancetta, diced
1 teaspoon olive oil
1 small onion, diced
2 cloves garlic, chopped
1 cup diced water-packed artichoke hearts
6 small red potatoes, boiled until tender, then quartered
1 tablespoon chopped fresh basil
10 eggs, lightly beaten
4 dashes Tabasco sauce
Salt and black pepper to taste
⅓ cup grated Parmesan cheese

Preheat oven to 350°. In a very large, nonstick, ovenproof sauté pan, cook the pancetta until golden brown. Add olive oil, onion, and garlic and sauté until you can smell the aroma, about 1 minute. Add artichoke hearts and potatoes and sauté lightly, about 2 minutes.

In a medium-size bowl, mix together basil, eggs, Tabasco, salt, and pepper. Add eggs to vegetable mixture in sauté pan, lifting the edges of the eggs with a rubber spatula until they just begin to set. Bake for 8 to 10 minutes, or until the eggs are set. Remove from oven and invert onto a plate and top with grated Parmesan cheese. Serve hot.

Sausage and Tomato Calzone

Makes 4 calzone

■ This is another variation on calzone. You will discover that you can stuff this dough with just about anything you enjoy eating.

1 tablespoon olive oil
1 medium onion, diced
3 cloves garlic, chopped
1 pound bulk Italian sausage
2 tomatoes, seeded and coarsely chopped
¼ cup diced sun-dried tomatoes
⅓ cup grated Parmesan cheese
⅓ cup grated mozzarella cheese
2 tablespoons chopped fresh basil
Salt and black pepper to taste
1 recipe Pizza Dough (see page 92)

In a large sauté pan, heat olive oil until very hot. Add onion and sauté until you can smell the aroma. Add the garlic and again sauté until you can smell the aroma. Add sausage and sauté until sausage is nearly cooked. Add tomatoes and sun-dried tomatoes and toss with sausage.

Heat mixture until bubbling hot. Remove from heat and place in a bowl to cool. Once the mixture is cool, mix in Parmesan and mozzarella cheeses, basil, salt, and pepper. Preheat oven to 375°. On a floured board, separate Pizza Dough into 4 equal pieces. Stretch or roll each piece out to a 6- to 8-inch circle about ¼ inch thick.

Divide sausage mixture among the dough circles, placing filling on one side of each circle. Fold dough over filling, forming a semicircle, and crimp well. Place on a baking sheet and bake for about 30 minutes, or until golden brown. Serve hot.

◆▪ Currant-Glazed Pork Chops ▪◆
with Blue Cheese Polenta

Serves 4

■ This dish is homey and comforting—definitely better than plain old pork chops! If you don't like blue cheese try another cheese like goat or aged Cheddar.

■ **PORK CHOPS**
4 pork chops, 8 ounces each
Salt and black pepper to taste
1 tablespoon olive oil

■ **BLUE CHEESE POLENTA**
2 cups Chicken Stock (see page 196)
3 cloves garlic, chopped
2 shallots, chopped
¾ cup finely ground cornmeal
2 ounces blue cheese
Salt and black pepper to taste

■ **CURRANT GLAZE**
3 cloves garlic, chopped
2 shallots, chopped
½ cup dry red wine
½ cup currant jelly
½ teaspoon cracked black pepper

For the pork chops, preheat oven to 350°. Season the chops with salt and pepper. Heat olive oil in a large, ovenproof sauté pan until smoking hot, add the chops, and brown on both sides over high heat, about 2 minutes on each side. Bake for 15 to 20 minutes, or until the pork chops reach an internal temperature of 145°.

While the pork chops are cooking, prepare the polenta. Place the chicken stock, garlic, and shallots in a medium-size saucepan. Bring to a boil over high heat. Slowly whisk in cornmeal so that it doesn't lump up. Cook the polenta over medium heat until the mixture is thick, 3 to 4 minutes. Add the cheese and mix well. Season with salt and pepper. Keep polenta warm while you finish the pork chops.

To glaze the pork chops, remove the pan from the oven and place over medium heat. Add the garlic and shallots and sauté lightly until you can smell the aroma. Add red wine and boil until reduced by half, 2 to 3 minutes. Add jelly and pepper and stir to coat the chops. Remove from heat and serve warm on a bed of the polenta.

Rack of Lamb
with Garlic and Peppercorn Crust

Serves 4

■ Make this dish when you really want to pull out all the stops and have a very special meal. Roast the garlic earlier in the day so you don't have to scramble around trying to get it to cook before you start the lamb.

> 2 tablespoons olive oil
> 2 sides rack of lamb, fat trimmed (6 bones each)
> 2 heads garlic, roasted (see page 198)
> 2 tablespoons green peppercorns
> 2 tablespoons pink peppercorns
> Kosher salt to taste
> 2 tablespoons cracked black pepper

Preheat oven to 350°. Heat oil in a large sauté pan until smoking hot. Place the racks in the pan, meat side down, and sear well. Turn and sear the other side. Remove pan from heat. Remove lamb from pan.

Remove roasted garlic from hull and rub on the meat side of the racks. Mix peppercorns and press into roasted garlic paste. Season with kosher salt and pepper. Return meat to pan and roast in oven for 15 to 20 minutes for medium-rare doneness. Remove from oven and allow to rest for 2 minutes before slicing. Serve hot.

Lamb Shanks
with Saffron and Ginger

Serves 4

■ Braised lamb shanks are some of the best comfort food to eat on a chilly winter evening. When you add exotic spices and aromatic herbs like saffron, ginger, and curry powder, this dish will do nothing but satisfy your taste buds. Serve with couscous.

4 lamb shanks, about 1 pound each
1 cup flour
1 tablespoon olive oil
3 cloves garlic, chopped
1 tablespoon chopped gingerroot
1 teaspoon orange juice concentrate
2 tablespoons rice vinegar
½ cup dry white wine
2 cups Lamb or Chicken Stock (see page 196)
1 large pinch saffron
1 teaspoon curry powder
Salt and black pepper to taste

Preheat oven to 350°. Dredge lamb shanks in flour to coat them. Heat olive oil in a large, ovenproof skillet until smoking hot. Add lamb shanks to pan and sear on both sides, about 2 minutes per side. Add garlic and gingerroot and sauté until you can smell the aroma. Add orange juice concentrate, vinegar, and wine and boil until reduced by half, about 3 to 5 minutes. Add stock, saffron, curry powder, salt, and pepper, and bring to a boil.

Cover pan, place in oven, and cook until lamb is tender, 1 to 1½ hours. Serve hot on a bed of couscous.

Roast Leg of Lamb

Serves 6

■ A simple roasted leg of lamb can be such a nice meal. Just remember to clean the leg as well as you can, because otherwise it will be tough. The longer the time and lower the temperature at which you cook the lamb, the more tender it will be. Serve with Caramelized Pearl Onions with Apple.

    3 pounds boneless leg of lamb
    Kosher salt
    Cracked black pepper
    1 tablespoon olive oil

Preheat oven to 300°. Clean the leg of lamb of most of the fat and silver skin. Tie the roast and season with salt and black pepper. Heat a roasting pan on the stovetop until smoking hot. Place lamb in roasting pan and sear well. Place in oven and roast slowly for 45 minutes to 1 hour for medium doneness. Let rest for 2 minutes before slicing.

Rack of Lamb with
Hazelnut Crust and
Mustard Seed Vinaigrette

Serves 4

■ Lamb is my favorite meat to cook. When I want to make a really special meal, I cook rack of lamb. To begin the meal I start with Warm Seafood Mousse with Fennel Salsa then finish with elegant Ginger Pear Galette. (Pictured opposite page 103.)

■ MUSTARD SEED VINAIGRETTE
¼ cup white wine
¼ cup mustard seeds
2 tablespoons sherry vinegar
2 cloves garlic, chopped
2 shallots, chopped
2 teaspoons Dijon-style mustard
½ teaspoon dry mustard
⅓ cup extra-virgin olive oil
1 teaspoon chopped fresh rosemary
Salt and black pepper to taste

■ RACK OF LAMB
2 racks of lamb, about 12 bones total, fat trimmed
Salt and black pepper to taste
1 tablespoon olive oil
1 tablespoon Dijon-style mustard
½ cup ground hazelnuts
½ cup bread crumbs
1 teaspoon chopped fresh rosemary

For the vinaigrette, place wine and mustard seeds in a small sauté pan and cook over high heat until the liquid is gone, 2 to 3 minutes. Remove the seeds from the pan and place in a bowl. Add vinegar, garlic, shallots, mustard, and dry mustard and mix well. Slowly whisk in olive oil until well blended. Add rosemary and season with salt and pepper. Set aside until ready to use.

For the lamb, preheat oven to 350°. Season the racks of lamb with salt and pepper. In a large, ovenproof sauté pan, heat oil until smoking hot. Place racks meat side down and sear well, about 2 minutes on high heat. Turn and sear the other side. Remove from the heat and, with a brush or the back of a spoon, smear the mustard over the lamb. In a small bowl, combine hazelnuts, bread crumbs, and rosemary. Press the mixture onto the lamb racks, packing it on well. Place back in the pan and roast for 15–20 minutes for medium-rare doneness (depending on thickness). The internal temperature should be about 135° on a meat thermometer. Remove from oven and allow to rest for 2 minutes before slicing. Slice and serve 3 bones per person. Drizzle each serving with Mustard Seed Vinaigrette.

Lamb Brochettes
with Cucumber-Garlic Sauce

Serves 6

■ You can skewer the lamb the night before and let the brochettes marinate. The sauce can also be prepared a day ahead. This sauce is also very nice with grilled vegetables or prawns.

■ CUCUMBER-GARLIC SAUCE
2 cups nonfat yogurt
4 cloves garlic, chopped
1 head roasted garlic (see page 198)
1 cucumber, grated
1 teaspoon finely chopped lemon zest
½ teaspoon ground cumin
1 teaspoon chopped fresh oregano
Salt and black pepper to taste

■ LAMB BROCHETTES
2 ½ pounds cubed lamb stew meat
3 cloves garlic, chopped
2 shallots, chopped
¼ cup red wine vinegar
Juice of 1 lemon
Zest of 1 lemon
2 teaspoons chopped fresh oregano
1 teaspoon chopped fresh thyme
½ cup extra-virgin olive oil
Black pepper to taste

For the cucumber sauce, place yogurt in a medium-size bowl. Add garlic, roasted garlic, cucumber, lemon zest, cumin, and oregano and mix well. Season the sauce with salt and pepper to taste. Refrigerate until ready to use. You can make this a day ahead of time if you like.

For the brochettes, place the cubed lamb in a large bowl. In medium-size bowl, mix garlic, shallots, vinegar, lemon juice, and zest. Add the oregano, thyme, olive oil, and pepper; mix well. Pour over the lamb and let marinade for 2 to 4 hours.

Light coals or start grill. Place lamb cubes on bamboo skewers, making 12 small skewers or 6 large ones. Grill the lamb for 3 to 4 minutes on each side for medium doneness. Serve hot with cucumber-garlic sauce.

Grilled Lamb Chops
with Maple Marinade

Serves 4

■ The marinade in this recipe can also be used on chicken breasts and even tuna fillets. Serve the chops with Thyme-Marinated Grilled Asparagus and try Pineapple Granita as a refreshing way to finish your meal.

3 shallots, chopped
3 cloves garlic, chopped
1 tablespoon chopped gingerroot
2 tablespoons rice vinegar
Juice of 1 lemon
Zest of 1 orange
1 teaspoon orange juice concentrate
½ cup maple syrup
¼ cup olive oil
¼ teaspoon chopped cilantro
½ teaspoon chopped fresh basil
1 teaspoon cracked black pepper
8 3-ounce lamb chops or 4 6-ounce chops
Salt to taste

For the marinade, mix shallots, garlic, gingerroot, vinegar, lemon, zest, and orange juice concentrate in a bowl or dish large enough to hold the chops. Add syrup and olive oil and mix again. Season with cilantro, basil, and pepper.

Place lamb chops in marinade, cover, and refrigerate for 1 to 3 hours. Oil grill rack and light coals or start grill. Remove lamb chops from marinade. Let the chops drain a bit before you grill them so that the marinade will not cause the coals to flare up. You can brush the chops with the leftover marinade while grilling.

Grill smaller chops for 3 or 4 minutes on each side for medium-rare to medium doneness. You may need to grill the 6-ounce chops a bit longer, depending on the thickness. Serve warm.

Sautéed Chicken Breasts
on a Bed of Lentils
with Lemon and Garlic

Serves 4

■ You can use the lentil salad as a bed for the chicken or as a side dish on its own. Toss the lentils with the dressing when they are warm so they absorb the flavor of the dressing better.

■ LENTIL SALAD
2½ cups cooked lentils
3 cloves garlic, chopped
2 shallots, chopped
Juice of 1 lemon
Zest of 1 lemon
2 tablespoons sherry vinegar
2 tablespoons chopped sun-dried tomatoes
⅓ cup extra-virgin olive oil
1 teaspoon chopped fresh oregano
Pinch ground cumin
Salt and black pepper to taste

■ SAUTÉED CHICKEN BREASTS
4 boneless chicken breasts, 6 ounces each
Salt and black pepper to taste
½ cup flour
1 tablespoon olive oil

For the lentil salad, place cooked lentils in a bowl. In another bowl combine garlic, shallots, lemon juice, zest, vinegar, and sun-dried tomatoes. Slowly whisk in olive oil until well blended. Season with oregano, cumin, salt, and pepper and mix well. Combine dressing with lentils and set aside while preparing the chicken.

For the chicken, preheat oven to 350°. Season chicken breasts with salt and pepper, then dredge them in flour to coat them.

Heat olive oil in a large sauté pan until smoking hot. Sear chicken on each side until golden brown, about 2 minutes per side. Bake for another 3 or 4 minutes, depending on the thickness of the chicken. Place the lentils on individual plates or on a tray. Place the chicken on top of the bed of lentils and serve hot.

◆· Braised Chicken ·◆
with Herbs and Shallots

Serves 4

■ People tend to stay away from certain cuts of meat because they are a bit tough. Chicken thighs are one of these, but when you braise them slowly with lots of herbs and shallots, they become tender and full of flavor, making a delicious, inexpensive meal. Serve the chicken on a bed of Hazelnut Mashed Potatoes.

> 4 chicken thighs
> ½ cup flour
> 2 tablespoons olive oil
> 6 shallots, coarsely chopped
> 3 cloves garlic, chopped
> ¼ cup dry red wine
> 2 tablespoons balsamic vinegar
> 1½ cups Chicken Stock (see page 196)
> 2 teaspoons chopped fresh rosemary
> 1 teaspoon chopped fresh thyme
> 1 teaspoon chopped fresh basil
> 1 teaspoon chopped fresh marjoram
> Salt and black pepper to taste

Preheat oven to 350°. Dredge chicken thighs in flour to coat. Heat olive oil in a large ovenproof sauté pan with a lid until smoking hot. Add shallots and allow to brown. Add chicken and sear on each side, about 2 minutes per side. Add garlic and sauté for about 1 minute, or until you can smell the aroma. Add wine and vinegar and boil until reduced by about half, 2 or 3 minutes. Add chicken stock, rosemary, thyme, basil, marjoram, salt, and pepper. Bring to a boil.

Cover and bake for 20 to 30 minutes, or until chicken is tender. Remove from oven and serve on a bed of Hazelnut Mashed Potatoes (see page 48). Spoon a bit of the sauce on top, and serve the rest on the side.

Polenta with Chicken, Arugula, and Goat Cheese

Serves 4

■ This is a dish we made for the cooking classes we teach. We wanted to make a dish that was like a pasta, but we didn't want to use pasta. The cubes of polenta work very well.

■ POLENTA CUBES
2 cups Chicken Stock (see page 196)
3 cloves garlic, chopped
¼ cup cayenne sauce
1 cup polenta or finely ground cornmeal
¼ cup grated Parmesan cheese
Salt and black pepper to taste

■ TO ASSEMBLE
4 cups polenta cubes
8 ounces boneless, skinless chicken breast
1 tablespoon olive oil
2 shallots, chopped
2 cloves garlic, chopped
1 cup Chicken Stock (see page 196)
¼ cup kalamata olives, pitted
¼ cup diced sun-dried tomatoes
¼ pound fresh arugula
¼ cup balsamic vinegar
2 teaspoons chopped fresh basil
Salt and black pepper to taste
½ cup soft, mild goat cheese, crumbled

For the polenta, place stock, garlic, and cayenne sauce in a saucepan and bring to a boil. Slowly whisk in the polenta and stir until the mixture is thick and resembles very thick mud, 4 to 5 minutes. Whisk in the Parmesan cheese and season well with salt and pepper. Pour onto a greased rimmed baking sheet and allow to cool in the refrigerator for about 1 hour. When polenta is cool, cut into ½-inch cubes and set aside.

To assemble the dish, cut the chicken breast into ½-inch slices. Heat oil in a large sauté pan until smoking hot. Add chicken and sear on both sides, about 2 minutes per side. Add shallots and garlic and sauté lightly, being careful not to burn them. Add stock and simmer to reduce, 2 to 3 minutes. Add olives and sun-dried tomatoes and cook for about 2 minutes. Add arugula and cook until it starts to wilt. Add polenta cubes and toss to mix. Add vinegar and basil. Season to taste. Add the goat cheese and toss to mix. Place on plates or a serving platter and top with more goat cheese or Parmesan cheese. Serve hot.

Sesame-Encrusted Chicken Breasts with Light Ginger-Soy Sauce

Serves 4

■ Serve this chicken on a bed of either steamed rice of couscous. Ginger, Carrot, and Daikon Salad is a good accompaniment. Be careful not to let the sesame crust burn when you are browning the chicken; that's why I call for finishing it in the oven.

■ SESAME-ENCRUSTED CHICKEN BREASTS
4 boneless, skinless chicken breasts, 6 ounces each
Salt and black pepper to taste
1 cup sesame seeds
½ teaspoon chile flakes
1 tablespoon vegetable oil

■ GINGER-SOY SAUCE
1 teaspoon vegetable oil
3 cloves garlic, chopped
1 tablespoon chopped gingerroot
½ cup mirin wine
1 cup Chicken Stock (see page 196)
1 tablespoon hoisin sauce
2 tablespoons Asian chile sauce
½ teaspoon dark sesame oil
½ teaspoon chopped fresh basil
Soy sauce to taste

Preheat oven to 350°. For the chicken breasts, season chicken with salt and pepper. In a small bowl, mix sesame seeds and chile flakes and then dredge the chicken breasts in the mixture to coat them. Heat vegetable oil in a large sauté pan until smoking hot. Add the chicken breasts and brown each side well, about 2 minutes per side.

Remove chicken from pan and transfer to a baking pan. Bake for another 3 to 5 minutes until the chicken breasts are just cooked through.

For the sauce, while the chicken breasts are baking, heat vegetable oil in the sauté pan you removed them from. Add garlic and gingerroot and sauté until you can smell the aroma, 1 to 2 minutes over high heat. Add mirin wine and boil over high heat until reduced by half, 2 to 3 minutes. Add chicken stock and boil over high heat to reduce a bit, 2 to 3 minutes.

If the chicken breasts are finished cooking by this time, remove them from the oven and allow to stand. Add hoisin sauce and chile sauce to sauté pan and bring to a boil. Season with sesame oil, basil, and soy sauce.

Serve chicken breasts over steamed rice or couscous. Serve half of the sauce over the chicken and the remainder on the side. This will not be a thick sauce; it is meant to be thin and light.

Chicken Pot Pie
with Cheese Crust

Serves 6

■ I would have to call this one of the ultimate comfort food dishes. It's an update of one of my favorite classic recipes that John and I make on rainy Sundays (which there are a lot of in Portland) when we want a cozy evening at home.

■ **CHEESE PASTRY**
1¼ cups flour
¼ cup finely grated sharp Cheddar cheese
2 tablespoons finely grated Parmesan cheese
½ cup shortening
1 teaspoon salt
6 tablespoons cold water

■ **FILLING**
4 skinless, boneless chicken breasts, 6 ounces each
3 medium carrots, diced
4 potatoes, diced
2 teaspoons olive oil
1 large onion, diced
4 cloves garlic, chopped
3 stalks celery, diced
½ cup white wine
⅓ cup dry sherry
1½ cups heavy cream
1 tablespoon chopped fresh tarragon
Zest of 1 lemon
1 teaspoon Dijon-style mustard
Salt and black pepper to taste

For the pastry, place flour, cheeses, shortening, and salt in a medium-size bowl and, with your fingertips, rub in the shortening until the mixture resembles a coarse meal. Add water and mix with a fork just until the mixture comes together. Form into a ball, wrap in plastic wrap, and allow to rest 30 minutes before rolling out.

For the filling, cut the chicken into large dice and place in a bowl. Add carrots and potatoes and mix well.

In a medium-size sauté pan, heat olive oil until very hot. Add onion, garlic, and celery and sauté just until you can smell the aroma. Remove from the heat and allow to cool, then add to the chicken mixture and mix well. Place in a deep 9-inch pie plate and refrigerate until the sauce is ready.

In a saucepan combine wine and sherry and boil over high heat to reduce until about ½ cup remains, 3 or 4 minutes. Add cream and reduce over high heat until 1 ½ cups of liquid remains, 4 or 5 minutes. Add tarragon, lemon zest, and mustard and simmer over low heat for another 5 minutes. Season with salt and pepper. Remove from heat and cool. Pour cooled sauce over chicken mixture.

Preheat oven to 425°. Roll the pastry out on a well-floured board to a circle about 10 inches in diameter and ¼ inch thick. Place over the filling and crimp the edge. If you like, you can cut shapes from the leftover dough and use them to decorate the top of the pie.

Bake for 15 minutes, then lower the oven temperature to 350° and bake for about 45 minutes more. Let the pie cool for about 5 minutes before serving.

Roast Turkey Breast
with Corn Bread and Walnut Stuffing

Serves 6

■ I have been doing holiday turkey this way for about five years now. You don't have to get up at the crack of dawn to stuff the turkey and put it in the oven: the whole process takes about two hours, including cooking time. A holiday during which you don't have to spend all day in the kitchen or deal with the turkey carcass—what a plan!

■ CORN BREAD AND WALNUT STUFFING

2 tablespoons unsalted butter
1 onion, diced
3 shallots, chopped
3 cloves garlic, chopped
3 stalks celery, diced
¾ cup dry sherry
1 cup diced French bread
1½ cup diced corn bread
½ cup wild rice, cooked
½ to 1 cup Chicken Stock (see page 196)
3 eggs
½ cup roughly chopped walnuts, toasted
2 teaspoons chopped fresh thyme, or 1 teaspoon dried
1 teaspoon chopped fresh oregano, or 1/2 teaspoon dried
1 teaspoon chopped fresh sage, or 1/2 teaspoon dried
½ teaspoon celery salt
Salt and black pepper to taste

■ TO ASSEMBLE

one boneless turkey breast, about 4 to 5 pounds, butterflied
    (see Glossary)
1½ tablspoons olive oil

To prepare the stuffing, heat butter in a large sauté pan over high heat until very hot. Be careful not to burn. Add onion, shallots, garlic, and celery, and sauté for 2 to 3 minutes, or until you can smell the aroma. Add sherry and cook until only about 2 tablespoons of liquid remain, about 3 minutes. Remove from the heat and allow to cool.

While the onion mixture is cooling place French bread, corn bread, and rice in a large bowl and toss to mix. When the onion mixture is room temperature, combine with the bread and rice mixture. Add enough chicken stock to moisten the bread well. Add eggs and mix well. Add walnuts, thyme, oregano, sage, celery salt, salt, and pepper, and mix thoroughly.

Preheat oven to 350°. To stuff the turkey, lay out turkey breast on a cutting board. Spread the stuffing evenly on the turkey to ½ inch from edge, roll the breast up, and tie securely with kitchen twine.

Heat olive oil in a large sauté pan until smoking hot. Place the turkey roll seam side down and sear the turkey well, about 4 to 5 minutes per side. Place in a baking dish and roast in oven about 35 to 45 minutes, or until the internal temperature reaches 155°. Allow to cool 2 to 3 minutes before removing kitchen twine, slicing, and placing on a serving platter.

Roasted Duck Legs ◼◼ with Wild Rice Pancakes

Serves 6

◼ Using kosher salt for the duck legs helps make the skin crispy. You can use the pancakes for other meals. Try them topped with smoked trout and a lemon sauce. (Pictured opposite page 118.)

◼ ROASTED DUCK LEGS
6 duck legs
Cracked black pepper
Kosher salt
1 tablespoon dried thyme

◼ WILD RICE PANCAKES
2 cups flour
1 tablespoon baking powder
1 teaspoon salt
2 cups cooked wild rice
2 cloves garlic, chopped
2 cups buttermilk
2 eggs, separated
1 tablespoon olive oil

For the duck legs, preheat oven to 375°. Place duck legs in a baking pan and season well with pepper, kosher salt, and thyme. Roast until the duck is very tender, 30 to 40 minutes. While duck is roasting, prepare the pancakes.

For the pancakes, place the flour, baking powder, salt, wild rice, and garlic in a large mixing bowl and mix well. Add buttermilk and egg yolks and mix well.

In a small bowl, whisk egg whites until they hold a soft peak. Gently fold into the rice mixture.

Heat oil on a griddle or in a large nonstick sauté pan. Add about 2 tablespoons of the batter to the hot pan to form 4- to 5-inch pancakes. Cook each pancake for about 2 minutes on each side. Keep pancakes warm while you are cooking the rest.

To serve, place two pancakes on each plate and top with a roasted duck leg. If you like, drizzle the duck with a bit of the pan juices. Serve hot.

Desserts

◼◆◼ Lacy Cafe Florentines ◼◆◼

Makes about 2 dozen

◼ These are very sophisticated cookies, especially when you serve them with fresh fruit or ice cream. If the cookies harden before you get a chance to shape them, put them back in the oven for about 30 seconds to soften them up a bit. If you like, you can drizzle the finished cookies with melted white chocolate.

> ¼ cup unsalted butter
> ⅓ cup brown sugar
> 2 tablespoons light corn syrup
> 2 tablespoons instant espresso powder
> Zest of 1 orange
> 2 tablespoons orange juice concentrate
> Dash pure vanilla extract
> ½ cup flour
> ½ cup toasted, ground hazelnuts

Preheat oven to 350°. In a medium-size saucepan, combine butter, sugar, and corn syrup and cook over medium heat, stirring constantly, until very smooth, 2 to 3 minutes. Add espresso, orange zest, orange juice concentrate, and vanilla and simmer for about 1 minute to dissolve the espresso powder. Remove from heat and stir in flour.

Drop heaping teaspoons onto a well-greased baking sheet. Top each cookie with some of the ground nuts. Bake for 10 to 12 minutes, or until golden brown and lacy.

Remove from oven and allow to stand for just under a minute. Remove cookies from pan with a spatula and place over a rolling pin to shape. This must be done before the cookies harden. Use wine bottles if you need more room. Let cookies cool on the rolling pin until they hold their shape, about 5 minutes.

Chocolate Truffle Tart

Serves 12

■ This is a tart that is best made a day ahead because it does have a few steps and you'll want to give yourself plenty of time so you're not stressed out before you serve dessert. Serve with whipped cream and, when berries are in season, top tart with blackberries or raspberries.

■ CRUST

2 cups chocolate cookie crumbs
¼ cup sugar
⅔ cup unsalted butter, melted

■ FILLING

14 ounces bittersweet chocolate
2 tablespoons unsalted butter
4 eggs, separated
¾ cup confectioners' sugar
¼ cup raspberry liqueur
Dash pure vanilla extract

■ GANACHE

6 ounces bittersweet chocolate
¾ cup heavy cream

For the crust, mix cookie crumbs and sugar in food processor. Add melted butter and mix well to incorporate. Press crumbs into a well-greased 9-inch flan or tart pan with a removable bottom. Refrigerate at least 30 minutes.

For the filling, place chocolate and butter in a metal bowl and melt over simmering water. Place egg yolks, sugar, liqueur, and extract in a metal bowl and cook over simmering water, whisking constantly. Cook until the mixture is thick and resembles softly whipped cream.

Remove crust from refrigerator and paint the bottom of the crust with about 2 ounces of the melted chocolate mixture. When the chocolate mixture and the egg mixture are about the same temperature, fold the chocolate into the egg mixture, using broad strokes.

Place egg whites in a clean mixer bowl and whip until they hold soft peaks. Fold egg whites into chocolate mixture, using broad strokes. Pour into crust and refrigerate for 1 hour.

For the ganache, place chocolate in a food processor and use short on-off pulses to break the pieces up a bit. Heat the cream in a small saucepan until it comes to a boil. Pour cream over chocolate in food processor and process until chocolate is smooth. Let cool for about 5 minutes. Pour ganache over top of tart. If you like, at this point you can top the tart with fresh berries. Refrigerate at least 1 hour more. Serve cold with whipped cream.

Almond Lemon Tart

Serves 12

■ Next to chocolate, lemon is my favorite flavor to use in desserts. I think this is a very elegant dessert: serve it after Rack of Lamb with Hazelnut Crust and Mustard Seed Vinaigrette. Top the tart with whipped cream.

■ **CRUST**
2 cups flour
½ cup confectioners' sugar
½ teaspoon salt
1 teaspoon almond extract
1 cup unsalted butter

■ **ALMOND LEMON FILLING**
1 cup almonds
½ cup almond paste
½ cup sugar
Juice of 1 lemon
Zest of 1 lemon
3 eggs
½ cup heavy cream
1 teaspoon almond extract

For the crust, preheat oven to 350°. Place flour, sugar, salt, and extract in a food processor. Cut the butter into pieces and, with the processor motor running, slowly drop in the butter, about 1 tablespoon at a time. Process until a ball of dough forms on top of the blade. Remove from processor and press into a greased 12-inch flan or tart pan with a removable bottom. Bake just until the crust sets, about 10 minutes. Set aside to cool.

For the filling, preheat oven to 350° if it is not heated already. Place almonds, almond paste, and sugar in a food processor and process to grind the nuts. Stop the machine and add juice, zest, eggs, cream, and extract. Process to blend well. Pour into the cooled crust and bake for 20 to 25 minutes, or until a knife inserted in the center comes out clean. Serve warm or cold with whipped cream.

White Chocolate–Hazelnut Macaroons

Makes 3 dozen

■ For these cookies, make sure that you whip the egg whites long enough. You want them to be stiff and shiny: if they are too soft the cookies will be runny and won't hold up when they are piped out. These cookies are good when you want a light dessert.

    5 egg whites
    ¾ cup sugar
    ½ teaspoon pure vanilla extract
    2 cups hazelnuts, toasted and finely ground
    4 ounces white chocolate, melted

Preheat oven to 350°. Place egg whites in a mixer bowl. Whip on full speed until foamy. Add sugar, a couple of tablespoons at a time. Whip until egg whites are shiny and hold a peak. Add vanilla. Gently fold in hazelnuts with big movements. Gently stir in melted chocolate. Place in a piping bag fitted with a star tube. Pipe 2-inch rosettes onto a baking sheet. Bake until golden brown, about 10 minutes.

Chocolate Truffles

Makes 18

■ These are perfect for a bit of chocolate after a large dinner. They are even better as a present for family or friends.

    12 ounces bittersweet chocolate, cut into pieces
    Zest of 1 orange
    1½ cups heavy cream
    2 tablespoons brandy
    1 cup Mexican cocoa powder

Place bittersweet chocolate in a food processor fitted with a metal blade. Add orange zest and process to chop the chocolate and zest. In a small saucepan, heat the cream until it just comes to a boil. With the processor turned off, add half the cream to the chocolate. Start the machine and add the rest of the cream. Process until the mixture is smooth. Remove mixture from processor and place in a shallow container. Stir in brandy and allow to chill until the chocolate is cool enough to handle and will hold its shape when rolled into a ball.

Scoop out a heaping spoonful of the mixture, roll it into a ball, and roll the truffle in cocoa powder. Place in a foil truffle cup. Repeat with remaining chocolate mixture. Serve at room temperature, or store in the refrigerator in an airtight container until ready to serve. Before serving, let truffles warm to room temperature.

Grilled Banana Compote

Serves 4

■ This is a fun dessert to serve in the winter: it just seems to bring a bit of sunshine into the house. If you have any way to cook this in front of your guests they will be impressed—just don't get carried away with the rum. Serve with ice cream.

2 large unpeeled bananas, cut in half
1 teaspoon vegetable oil
1 tablespoon unsalted butter
¼ cup brown sugar
¼ cup dark rum
Splash Grand Marnier
1 teaspoon ground cinnamon
½ teaspoon ground ginger
Orange zest, for garnish

Rub the cold grill rack with oil, and light coals or start grill. Brush bananas with vegetable oil and grill for 2 to 3 minutes. Remove from the grill, peel, and cut into medium-size pieces. In a medium-size sauté pan, heat butter until bubbling. Add brown sugar and bring to a boil. Add banana pieces and rum. Splash with Grand Marnier. Boil for about 1 minute. Add cinnamon and ginger; remove from heat. Serve warm over ice cream, garnished with orange zest.

Bistro Faux Soufflés

Makes 6 soufflés

■ This is a recipe that my husband John invented. It has all the style and look—and none of the hassles—of a real chocolate soufflé. When you carry these to the table, everyone will oooh and ahhhh. (Pictured opposite page 119.)

½ cup unsalted butter, softened
2¼ cups brown sugar
3 eggs
12 ounces bittersweet chocolate, melted
1 cup hot espresso
2 cups flour
2 teaspoons baking soda
Pinch salt
1 cup sour cream
1 teaspoon pure vanilla extract

Preheat oven to 350°. In a large mixing bowl, cream butter and sugar until fluffy. Add eggs, one at a time, mixing well after each addition. Add melted chocolate and espresso and mix well.

In a small bowl, mix flour, baking soda, and salt. Add half of the sour cream to the chocolate mixture and mix well. Add half the flour mixture and mix again. Repeat. Add vanilla and mix.

Grease six 8-ounce ramekins and fit with foil collars. Distribute the batter among the ramekins. Bake for 25 to 30 minutes, or until a knife inserted in the center comes out clean. Serve warm.

Poached Ginger Cheesecake

Serves 12

■ You will love the way this cheesecake feels in your mouth—both rich and light in the same instant. This is now the way I make all my cheesecake recipes—I really can't go back to the traditional heavy, rich cheesecake. One word of caution: don't underbake or it will just be gooey.

> 2 tablespoons chopped crystallized ginger
> 2 pounds cream cheese
> 1½ cups sugar
> ½ teaspoon pure vanilla extract
> 3 eggs
> 2 egg yolks
> 2 egg whites

Preheat oven to 350°. In a food processor, purée candied ginger. Add cream cheese and sugar and process until very smooth. Stop machine and scrape the sides to help the mixture purée. Add vanilla, whole eggs, and egg yolks. Process to mix. Transfer mixture to a medium-size bowl.

In a small bowl, whip egg whites until they hold soft peaks. Fold gently into the cream cheese mixture.

Line a 2-quart metal bowl with plastic wrap. Place batter in bowl. Cover bowl with plastic wrap. Place the bowl in a larger bowl, then fill the larger bowl about half full with hot water. Cover with foil. Bake for about 1 hour, or until cheesecake moves as one when jiggled (don't worry about the plastic wrap—it will hold up fine in the oven!). Chill, unmold onto a plate, and serve cold.

Mini Chocolate Cakes
with White Chocolate Lava

Serves 6

■ These cakes are more like brownies, with a chunk of white chocolate in the middle of each. They are really at their best when served warm.

1 cup unsalted butter, softened
½ cup sugar
3 eggs
3 egg yolks
1 pound bittersweet chocolate, melted
1 cup flour
1 cup toasted, ground pecans
1 teaspoon pure vanilla extract
6 ounces white chocolate, in 1-ounce pieces
¾ cup heavy cream, whipped
2 ounces bittersweet chocolate, grated

Preheat oven to 350°. Using an electric mixer with a whisk attachment, cream butter and sugar together on high speed until light and fluffy, about 5 minutes. Add eggs and egg yolks, one at a time, mixing well after each addition. Continue to mix until the egg mixture is lemon colored, about 3 minutes more. Lower the mixer speed and add the melted chocolate. Stop and scrape down the sides and then continue to mix. Add flour, nuts, and vanilla and mix just until the batter comes together.

Distribute the batter among six 8-ounce well-greased ramekins. Place the ramekins on a baking sheet and bake for 15 minutes. Remove from oven. Place a 1-ounce piece of white chocolate into the middle of each half-baked cake. Return cakes to oven and bake for another 10 to 15 minutes, or until a knife inserted in the side comes out clean. Do not insert the knife into the center or you will hit the white chocolate.

Let cakes cool for about 10 minutes, then invert onto a plate and pipe whipped cream on the top of each cake. Top with grated chocolate and serve warm.

Buttermilk Cake
with Crème Fraîche

Serves 12

■ Serve this cake warm out of the oven with the crème fraîche, then top with seasonal berries or fruit. You can also toast and grind some nuts to sprinkle on top—and even shred chocolate on top of that!

■ CRÈME FRAÎCHE
2 cups heavy cream
2 tablespoons sour cream
⅓ cup confectioners' sugar

■ BUTTERMILK CAKE
2 cups unsalted butter
2½ cups sugar
6 eggs
3½ cups flour
1 cup buttermilk
1 teaspoon pure vanilla extract
Zest of 1 lemon
⅓ cup orange liqueur

■ GARNISH
2 pints raspberries
2 pints blackberries or marionberries
½ cup confectioners' sugar

For the crème fraîche, in a small bowl combine cream and sour cream; mix well. Cover and let sit at room temperature overnight. Refrigerate. When cold, whisk in confectioners' sugar.

For the cake, preheat oven to 350°. Dice butter and place in a mixer bowl or food processor. Add sugar and mix until the mixture is light and fluffy, about 5 minutes. Add eggs, one at a time, mixing well after each addition. Add flour, a third at a time, mixing after each addition. Add buttermilk, vanilla, and zest, and mix. Pour batter into a well-greased and floured bundt pan. Bake for 50 to 60 minutes, or until a knife inserted in the center comes out clean. Remove from oven and sprinkle with orange liqueur. Let cool.

To serve, slice cake and drizzle with crème fraîche, then distribute berries over the slices and dust with confectioners' sugar. The cake is best eaten warm.

Chocolate Crème Caramel

Serves 6

■ Let this crème caramel sit for a while before serving so it has a chance to make the caramel sauce: I suggest making it a day before you want to serve it.

    1¼ cups sugar
    ⅓ cup water
    ½ cup toasted, roughly chopped hazelnuts
    2 cups half-and-half
    4 ounces bittersweet chocolate
    3 whole eggs
    3 egg yolks
    ½ teaspoon pure vanilla extract

Preheat oven to 350°. Place ¾ cup of the sugar and the ⅓ cup water in a medium-size saucepan and cook over high heat until the sugar is golden brown. Do not stir until the sugar starts to brown, then you may stir to even the color. Distribute the toasted hazelnuts among 6 ramekins, then pour in the caramelized sugar and allow to set while you make the custard.

Over a double boiler or in a microwave oven, heat half-and-half with chocolate just until the chocolate is melted. Place the eggs and yolks in a bowl. Add a bit of the half-and-half mixture to the eggs to temper them, then pour the eggs into the half-and-half mixture and whisk well to blend. Add the remaining ½ cup sugar and the vanilla and mix well.

Pour custard into prepared cups. Place ramekins in a baking dish and fill the dish halfway up the sides of the ramekins with hot water. Place in oven and bake just until the custard is set or until a knife inserted in the center comes out clean. Remove from the water bath and cool slightly, then refrigerate for at least 2 to 4 hours before serving; overnight is best. Run a knife around the edges of the ramekins and invert onto individual plates. Serve cold.

Cappuccino Cream Pie

Serves 12

■ I designed this pie to be a grown-up version of a childhood favorite, chocolate cream pie. The addition of macadamia nuts in the crust and white chocolate in the filling makes this version a bit more sophisticated than the pie you may have enjoyed as a child.

■ MACADAMIA CRUST

1½ cups graham cracker crumbs
¾ cup toasted, ground macadamia nuts
⅓ cup sugar
1 teaspoon ground cinnamon
½ teaspoon ground nutmeg
3 tablespoons unsalted butter, melted

■ CAPPUCCINO FILLING

3 cups milk
½ cup sugar
⅓ cup flour
5 ounces white chocolate, cut into small pieces
3 tablespoons instant espresso powder
Dash pure vanilla extract
5 egg yolks
1½ cups heavy cream, whipped until stiff
Chocolate-covered espresso beans, for garnish

For the crust, in a large bowl combine crumbs, nuts, sugar, cinnamon, and nutmeg and mix well. Add butter and mix well to moisten the nut mixture. Press the mixture into a well-greased 12-inch flan or tart pan with a removable bottom. Chill for 30 minutes.

For the filling, place milk, sugar, and flour in a heavy-bottomed saucepan and mix well so that there are no lumps. Add the chocolate, espresso powder, and vanilla. Cook, stirring, over medium heat until mixture is thick enough to coat the back of a spoon.

Place the egg yolks in a small bowl and whisk in enough of the milk mixture to warm the yolks up to the temperature of the milk. Pour the yolk mixture into the saucepan and cook, stirring, over medium heat until very thick. Pour into the prepared crust and refrigerate for at least 2 to 3 hours. Just before serving, top with whipped cream and garnish with chocolate-covered espresso beans. Serve chilled.

Chocolate Hazelnut Tart

Serves 12

■ This tart is sort of like a flourless brownie in a chocolate crust. Substitute another type of nut if you can't find hazelnuts. Serve this dessert after a light meal, such as White Bean–Pancetta Soup. I like to top it with softly whipped cream.

■ CRUST
1½ cups flour
½ cup unsweetened cocoa powder
½ cup confectioners' sugar
1 teaspoon pure vanilla extract
½ teaspoon salt
1 cup unsalted butter, softened

■ FILLING
12 ounces bittersweet chocolate, cut into pieces
2 tablespoons unsalted butter
4 eggs
1 cup toasted, ground hazelnuts
3 tablespoons hazelnut liqueur

■ TOPPING
1 cup Ganache (see pages 132–133)

For the crust, preheat oven to 350°. Place flour, cocoa powder, confectioners' sugar, vanilla, and salt in a mixer bowl or food processor bowl. With the machine running, add the butter, about 1 tablespoon at a time. Mix until the dough forms into a ball.

Press dough into a 12-inch flan or tart pan with a removable bottom. Bake for about 10 minutes. Remove from oven and allow to cool.

For the filling, preheat oven to 350°, if it is not heated already. Place chocolate and butter in a metal bowl and place over a pan of simmering water. Do not allow the bottom of the bowl to touch the water. Stir until chocolate and butter are melted. Add eggs and nuts to chocolate mixture and mix well. Add hazelnut liqueur and mix.

Pour mixture into crust and bake for 20 to 30 minutes, or until a knife inserted in the center comes out clean. Remove from oven and allow to cool.

When tart is cool, pour ganache over the top and spread evenly. Refrigerate for at least 2 hours before serving. Slice and serve with softly whipped cream.

Polenta Orange Cake
with Almond Glaze

Serves 12

■ This cake has a light texture, and the cornmeal gives it a bit of crunchiness. The syrup soaks into the cake, keeping it moist. It's best served warm.

■ POLENTA ORANGE CAKE
½ cup unsalted butter
½ cup sugar
2 eggs
5 egg yolks
1 tablespoon orange juice concentrate
Zest of 1 orange
¾ cup flour
½ cup cornmeal
1 tablespoon baking powder
Pinch salt

■ ALMOND GLAZE
½ cup water
½ cup sugar
¼ cup almond liqueur
1 orange, cut in half

For the cake, preheat oven to 350°. Place butter and sugar in mixer bowl and cream, using an electric mixer on high speed. Add the egg and yolks, one at a time, mixing well after each addition. After the eggs are incorporated, mix on high speed until the mixture is light and fluffy, about 5 minutes. With the mixer on low speed, add orange juice concentrate and zest; mix well.

In a medium-size bowl, combine flour, cornmeal, baking powder, and salt; add to the egg mixture. Pour into a springform pan lined with foil and bake for 30 minutes, or until cake springs back when touched. Remove from the oven. Brush with Almond Glaze while cake is still warm.

For the glaze, while the cake is baking, place water, sugar, liqueur, and orange in the medium-size saucepan and cook over high heat until mixture is thick and syrupy, 5 to 8 minutes. Remove the orange and allow to cool slightly before brushing the warm cake generously with the glaze.

Ginger Mascarpone Cream Cake

Serves 6

■ This is more like a sandwich than a cake. When you make the génoise, be sure to use big strokes when mixing the flour. The whipped eggs are the leavening agent, and if you beat them too much you will get a flat sponge cake.

■ GINGER GÉNOISE
5 large eggs
1 cup sugar
1 teaspoon ground ginger
2 teaspoons minced crystallized ginger
½ teaspoon pure vanilla extract
1¼ cups flour
1 tablespoon butter, melted

■ MASCARPONE CREAM FILLING
8 ounces white chocolate
1½ cups mascarpone cheese
1 teaspoon ground cinnamon
2 tablespoons dark rum

■ GARNISH
½ cup confectioners' sugar
¾ cup heavy cream, whipped
1 tablespoon diced crystallized ginger

For the cake, preheat oven to 350°. Place eggs, sugar, ground and crystallized ginger, and vanilla in a metal mixing bowl and place over simmering water.

Heat eggs until warm to the touch, about 100°. Place bowl on mixer fitted with a whip attachment and whip on high speed until eggs have tripled in volume, about 5 minutes. Remove bowl from mixer. In three parts, using large movements, fold in flour alternately with melted butter. Pour batter into a well-greased and floured 9 by 11-inch baking pan. Bake until cake is golden brown and springs back when touched, about 20 to 30 minutes. Remove from oven and allow to cool 10 to 15 minutes. Invert the cake onto a clean board and cut into 12 rectangles. Set aside.

For the filling, melt the white chocolate over very low heat. Remove chocolate from heat and allow to cool slightly. Fold mascarpone cheese into white chocolate. Add cinnamon and rum and mix. Chill the filling for about 1 hour, or until firm.

To assemble, spread chilled filling over six of the cake rectangles. Top with a second slice of cake. Sprinkle confectioners' sugar over the top, then pipe whipped cream on the sides of the cake, and top the cream with ginger. Serve cold.

Lemon Cookies

Makes 2 dozen

■ Enjoy these cookies in a quiet moment in the afternoon or as a dessert after a summer luncheon. Kids will even enjoy taking them in their lunchboxes to school. They won't trade these away!

■ COOKIES
½ cup sugar
½ cup unsalted butter
1 teaspoon pure vanilla extract
Zest of 1 lemon
3 eggs
2¼ cups flour
2 teaspoons baking powder
Pinch salt

■ FROSTING
1 tablespoon unsalted butter
2 tablespoons cream cheese
Juice of 1 lemon
½ teaspoon pure vanilla extract
3 cups confectioners' sugar

For the cookies, preheat oven to 350°. Place sugar and butter in a mixer bowl and, using an electric mixer, cream on high speed until fluffy and lemon colored. Add vanilla and zest and mix. Add eggs, one at a time, mixing well after each addition. In a medium-size bowl, mix flour, baking powder, and salt. Add to the butter mixture and mix until well blended.

Roll dough out ¼ inch thick and cut shapes with cookie cutters. Place on a greased baking sheet and bake until golden brown, 10 to 12 minutes. Remove from pan and allow to cool. While the cookies are cooling, make the frosting.

For the frosting, in a food processor or with an electric mixer, mix butter and cream cheese until blended and softened. Add lemon and vanilla and mix well. Add confectioners' sugar and mix well. Use to frost the cookies.

Chocolate Pâté
with Dried Apricots

Serves 12

■ This chocolate pâté is like a dense mousse, dark and intensely rich. Serve very small slices because it is so rich. Top each slice with some softly whipped cream. I like to enjoy this dessert with a rich shot of espresso.

>1 pound bittersweet chocolate, cut into pieces
>½ cup unsalted butter
>2 tablespoons brandy
>4 eggs, separated
>¼ cup sugar
>1 cup heavy cream
>1 cup toasted, ground hazelnuts
>½ cup diced dried apricots

Place chocolate and butter in a metal bowl over simmering water and melt. Do not allow the bottom of the bowl to touch the water. Let the chocolate mixture cool for a moment, then add brandy and egg yolks and stir well.

In a clean mixing bowl, beat the egg whites until foamy, then add sugar, 1 tablespoon at a time, beating until the whites hold a soft peak.

In another mixing bowl, whip the cream until it holds soft peaks. Fold a small amount of the whipped cream into the chocolate mixture, then fold in the rest of the cream. Gently fold in egg whites.

Pour the pâté into a loaf pan lined with plastic wrap. Top with toasted hazelnuts and dried apricots and refrigerate for at least 4 hours. Remove from the pan and cut into thin slices with a hot knife. Serve with whipped cream.

SEASONAL FRUIT DESSERTS

Roasted Duck Legs with
Wild Rice Pancakes (page 128)

Bistro Faux Soufflés (page 138)

Ricotta Cheesecake with
Marinated Fruit (page 152)

Peach Gratin (page 163)

Ginger Pear Galette (page 164)

Meringue Shortcakes with
Blueberries (page 171)

Prosciutto Breakfast Strata
(page 182)

Spiced Pecan French Toast
(page 183)

Walnut-Stuffed Apples

Serves 4

■ Make sure you do not overcook the apples or they will explode all over your oven. As always, you can use different nuts if you like. Also, if you have a hard time finding mascarpone cheese you can substitute more cream cheese.

> 1 cup toasted walnuts
> ¼ cup mascarpone cheese
> ¼ cup cream cheese
> ⅔ cup brown sugar
> ½ teaspoon pure vanilla extract
> 2 tablespoons dark rum
> 1 teaspoon ground cinnamon
> ½ teaspoon ground ginger
> ¼ teaspoon ground nutmeg
> ¼ teaspoon ground cloves
> ¼ teaspoon ground allspice
> 4 Granny Smith apples

Place toasted walnuts in a food processor. Process to coarsely chop the nuts. Add mascarpone cheese, cream cheese, brown sugar, vanilla, and rum. Process to mix. Stop the machine and add cinnamon, ginger, nutmeg, cloves, and allspice. Process again to mix. Set aside in the refrigerator until ready to use.

Preheat oven to 350°. Slice about ¼ inch from the tops of the apples. Remove the core. Scoop a bit of the apple out. Plug the bottom of the apple with the bottom of the core. Stuff each apple with a little over ⅓ cup of the walnut mixture. Place apples in a well-greased shallow baking pan. Bake about 40 minutes, or until apples are fork-tender. Serve warm.

Ricotta Cheesecake with Marinated Fruit

Serves 12

■ Ricotta cheesecakes have a lighter texture than traditional cheesecakes. To go with this feeling, use any seasonal fruit you like. (Pictured opposite 134.)

■ CHEESECAKE
1 pound cream cheese
2 cups ricotta cheese
1 cup sugar
4 eggs
Zest of 1 lemon
1 teaspoon pure vanilla extract

■ MARINATED FRUIT
1 pint strawberries, hulled and cut in half
½ cup blackberries
1 cantaloupe, peeled, seeded, and diced
½ cup sweet white wine
¼ cup sugar
Zest of 1 orange
Dash pure vanilla extract
Pinch nutmeg

■ ACCOMPANIMENT
Softly whipped cream

For the cheesecake, preheat oven to 350°. Grease a 10-inch springform pan and line with foil. Process cream cheese in a food processor until smooth. Add ricotta cheese and process just to combine. Add sugar and process to combine. With the motor running, add eggs, one at a time. Add lemon zest and vanilla and mix well.

Pour into prepared pan. Place in oven and bake for 40 to 50 minutes, or until a knife inserted in the center comes out clean. Let cheesecake cool in the refrigerator for at least 2 hours before serving.

For the marinated fruit, place fruit in a large bowl and set aside. In a small saucepan, combine wine, sugar, orange zest, vanilla, and nutmeg and place over high heat. Bring mixture to a boil and cook, stirring only once, for about 5 minutes to thicken the syrup. Remove from the heat and allow to cool 5 minutes.

Pour syrup over fruit and allow to marinate for 30 minutes in the refrigerator. Serve with the cheesecake and softly whipped cream.

Marionberry Pie
with Hazelnut Crust

Serves 12

■ Be careful when you handle the crust for this pie: the nuts make it a little more delicate. If you can't find marionberries in your area then substitute blackberries or raspberries. I love to eat this pie just out of the oven with vanilla ice cream.

■ HAZELNUT CRUST
2½ cups flour
⅓ toasted, ground hazelnuts
½ teaspoon salt
⅓ cup shortening
⅓ cup unsalted butter
Dash pure vanilla extract
7 to 8 tablespoons cold water

■ MARIONBERRY FILLING
2½ cups marionberries
1 cup sugar
2 tablespoons cornstarch
Grated zest of 1 lemon
1 teaspoon ground cinnamon
2 tablespoons unsalted butter

For the crust, place flour, hazelnuts, and salt in a medium-size bowl. Add shortening, butter, and vanilla extract to the flour mixture and rub between your fingertips until mixture resembles coarse meal. With a fork, mix in just enough water to make the dough come together. Add water a little at a time; each time you make this the amount of water will change depending on the weather.

Wrap the dough in plastic wrap and allow it to stand for 30 minutes. Cut dough in half and roll out on a floured board into two 12-inch circles; set aside.

For the filling, preheat oven to 425°. Place one circle of dough in a 12-inch pie pan. Combine berries, sugar, cornstarch, zest, and cinnamon in a medium-size bowl and toss to mix well. Pour the berry mixture into the prepared crust. Cut the butter into small pieces and dot filling with butter. Top with the second circle of crust and crimp the edges to seal. Prick the dough with a fork and bake in preheated oven for 15 minutes. Reduce heat to 350° and bake for about 30 minutes, or until golden brown. Remove pie from oven and allow it to sit for 15 to 20 minutes before serving. Serve with vanilla ice cream.

Strawberry-Rhubarb Tart

Serves 12

■ Sometimes the rhubarb can keep this tart from setting up properly. If you have this problem, try sautéing the rhubarb in butter until it's just a little soft, then remove from the liquid and add to the berries. The tart's texture should be soft and creamy, but not liquid. Serve with ice cream or softly whipped cream.

■ CRUST

1½ cups flour
½ teaspoon salt
¼ cup shortening
¼ cup unsalted butter
About 6 tablespoons cold water
½ cup toasted, ground almonds
Zest of 1 orange
¼ cup sugar

■ FILLING

2 pints strawberries, hulled and cut in half
1½ cups finely diced rhubarb
1½ cups sugar
¼ cup heavy cream
3 eggs
1 egg yolk
½ teaspoon pure vanilla extract

For the crust, place flour and salt in a bowl. Add shortening and butter. Rub mixture between your fingers until it resembles coarse meal. Stir with a fork, drizzling water into the dough just until it comes together. Wrap and set aside for 15 minutes.

Roll dough out into a 9 by 11-inch rectangle on a well-floured board. Sprinkle two-thirds of dough with ground nuts, zest, and sugar. Fold the clean side of the dough over one-third of the nut-covered dough. Then fold the last third over. Allow to rest for 15 to 20 minutes. While dough is resting, preheat oven to 350°. Roll out again on a well-floured board to a 12-inch circle. Place in a 12-inch flan or tart pan with removable bottom. Bake for about 15 minutes. Set aside to cool.

For the filling, place strawberries on bottom of crust. Place rhubarb and ½ cup of the sugar in a large sauté pan and cook until the rhubarb is crisp-tender. Let cool slightly. Pour over the strawberries. In a bowl, combine cream, eggs, egg yolk, remaining 1 cup sugar, and vanilla and mix well. Pour over berry mixture. Bake for 25 to 30 minutes, or until the custard is set. Serve warm with ice cream or softly whipped cream.

■◆ Pumpkin Tart ◆■

Serves 12

■ This is my take on traditional pumpkin pie. For years I put nuts on the top of my pie, but when I went to cut it the crispy texture on top of the soft custard made each piece look terrible. So I got the idea that I could put the nuts in the crust so I have a crispy texture on the bottom and soft custard on top: delicious! Serve with ice cream or whipped cream, as you would any pumpkin pie.

■ CRUST
2 cups toasted pecans
¼ cup sugar
3 tablespoons butter, melted
½ teaspoon ground cinnamon

■ FILLING
1½ cups pumpkin purée
3 eggs
½ cup brown sugar
1 cup half-and-half
1 teaspoon ground cinnamon
1 teaspoon ground ginger
½ teaspoon ground allspice
½ teaspoon ground nutmeg
½ teaspoon ground cloves
1 tablespoon finely chopped crystallized ginger
1 teaspoon pure vanilla extract

For the crust, place pecans and sugar in a food processor and process until the nuts are a coarse meal. Add butter and cinnamon and process just to mix. Press into a well-greased 12-inch flan or tart pan with a removable bottom. Refrigerate for at least 30 minutes.

For the filling, preheat oven to 350°. Place pumpkin in a large mixing bowl. Add eggs and mix well. Mix in sugar, then half-and-half. Add cinnamon, ground ginger, allspice, nutmeg, cloves, crystallized ginger, and vanilla and mix well. Pour into prepared crust. Bake until the pumpkin filling is set and a knife inserted into the center comes out clean, about 25 to 30 minutes. Let cool a bit and serve with whipped cream or ice cream.

◼︎▲ Phyllo Purses Stuffed ▲◼︎
with Raspberries and Mascarpone Cheese

Serves 4

◼︎ This is a dessert that John and I made for 400 at the International Pinot Noir Festival, so I obviously think it would be a great dessert for you to serve to a large group of people. (Well, maybe not quite 400.) Serve with softly whipped cream.

    1 cup mascarpone cheese
    ¼ cup chopped walnuts
    ¼ cup sugar
    1 pint fresh raspberries
    12 sheets phyllo dough
    ½ cup butter, melted

Preheat oven to 350°. Place cheese, walnuts, and sugar in a medium-size mixing bowl. Fold in the raspberries. Set aside. Unfold the sheets of phyllo dough and cut them into thirds. Remove 3 sheets of phyllo and brush each with butter. Stack the sheets one on top of another. Place one-fourth of the berry mixture in the middle of the phyllo. Gather the edges of the phyllo up, twisting to form a "kiss." Place on a greased baking sheet. Make three more complete purses. Bake for 15 to 20 minutes, until golden brown. Serve warm with softly whipped cream.

Strawberry Shortcake

Serves 6

■ Like many of my recipes with a classical base, this has a little twist. This will remind you of your childhood, but it is just a bit more sophisticated than the strawberry shortcake you remember.

■ **SHORTCAKE**
2 cups flour
2 tablespoons sugar
½ teaspoon salt
1 tablespoon baking powder
1 teaspoon diced crystallized ginger
½ teaspoon ground ginger
½ teaspoon almond extract
¼ cup unsalted butter, diced
½ cup plus 2 tablespoons milk

■ **TO ASSEMBLE**
2 pints strawberries, hulled
1½ cups heavy cream
¼ cup sugar

For the shortcake, preheat oven to 350°. In a medium-size bowl, combine flour, sugar, salt, baking powder, crystallized and ground ginger, and almond extract. Add butter and rub in with your fingertips to form a coarse meal. Add milk and mix with a fork just until the dough comes together. On a floured board, roll dough out to a thickness of about ½ inch. Cut 6 triangles from the dough, or use a cookie cutter to cut any shape you like. Place on a greased baking sheet and bake for about 20 minutes, or until golden brown.

To assemble the shortcake, cut the larger berries in halves or quarters. Whip cream with about ¼ cup sugar until it will hold a peak. Split the shortcakes and place on plates. Top the bottom halves with whipped cream and berries and place the other half on top. Top with more whipped cream and berries. Serve.

Spiced Apple Sorbet

Makes 2 cups

■ This doesn't have the smooth texture that some sorbets have—you can actually feel little bits of apple. A bit of softly whipped cream with fresh grated nutmeg is a perfect way to garnish this sorbet.

> 1 cup apple cider
> 3 Granny Smith apples, peeled, cored, and diced
> ½ cup sugar
> ½ teaspoon pure vanilla extract
> 1 teaspoon ground cinnamon
> ½ teaspoon ground ginger
> ½ teaspoon ground allspice
> ½ teaspoon ground nutmeg
> Pinch ground cloves

Place all ingredients in a medium-size saucepan and bring to a boil. Cook over medium heat until apples are fork-tender. Remove from heat and purée. Freeze in ice cream maker, following manufacturer's instructions.

Puff Pastry Fruit Tart

Serves 12

■ If you can't find mascarpone cheese you can substitute cream cheese softened with a bit of cream. Serve with whipped cream, and take advantage of fresh seasonal berries to top this tart. You can cut the tart in different shapes or even make little, individual tarts—bake them just until they are golden brown.

½ recipe Quick Puff Pastry (see page 202)
1½ cups mascarpone cheese
½ cup sugar
1 teaspoon orange juice concentrate
Zest of 1 orange
2 pints fresh berries

Preheat oven to 350°. Roll pastry out on a well-floured board to a rectangle about 18 by 9 inches. Cut a ½-inch strip off each side. Place along the top edges of the pastry rectangle to form a frame. Bake for 20 minutes, until golden brown.

When cool, remove some of the pastry layers in the middle of the shell, or press the middle down to form an indentation. In a small bowl, combine mascarpone cheese, sugar, orange juice concentrate, and orange zest. Mix well. Spread in middle of tart shell. Cover with fresh berries. Chill. Serve cold with whipped cream.

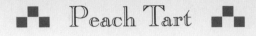 Peach Tart

Serves 12

■ This is my favorite crust. Sometimes I press the dough out to a quarter of an inch thick, cut it into triangles, bake it, and serve it as cookies. With the peach filling and topped with whipped cream or caramel sauce, it's a really good dessert.

■ TART PASTRY
2 cups flour
2 tablespoons chopped crystallized ginger
½ cup brown sugar
1 teaspoon pure vanilla extract
½ teaspoon salt
1 cup unsalted butter, softened

■ PEACH FILLING
5 or 6 large peaches, peeled and sliced
¾ cup cream cheese
½ cup heavy cream
1 cup sugar
4 eggs
½ teaspoon ground cinnamon
Pinch ground allspice
Pinch ground nutmeg
½ teaspoon rum extract

For the pastry, preheat oven to 350°. Place flour, ginger, sugar, vanilla, and salt in a food processor. Cut butter into 1- to 2-tablespoon pieces and, with the machine running, add the pieces to processor, one at a time. Process until a ball of dough forms on top of the blade. Remove from machine.

Press into a well-greased 12-inch flan or tart pan with removable bottom. Bake for about 10 minutes, just until the dough starts to set. Remove from oven and cool while making the filling.

For the filling, preheat oven to 350°, if you haven't done so already. Arrange sliced peaches in concentric circles in cooled tart shell, filling the shell. In a food processor, place cream cheese, cream, and sugar and mix until smooth. Add eggs, one at a time, mixing well after each addition. Add cinnamon, allspice, nutmeg, and rum extract and mix well. Pour over peaches and bake for about 30 minutes, or until a knife inserted in the center comes out clean. Serve warm or cold with softly whipped cream or caramel sauce.

◆▪ Mangoes with ▪◆
White Chocolate Mousse

Serves 6 to 8

■ With mangoes, this dessert has a tropical flair, but if you can't find really good mangoes try peaches or fresh berries. This is really pretty in a large wine glass, or fan the mango out on a dessert plate, then top with the mousse.

■ WHITE CHOCOLATE MOUSSE

6 eggs yolks
1 cup confectioners' sugar
¼ cup dark rum
Dash pure vanilla extract
1 pound white chocolate, melted
1½ cups heavy cream, whipped

■ TO ASSEMBLE

6 to 8 ripe mangoes, peeled and diced
2 dashes almond Italian syrup
Fresh mint, for garnish

For the mousse, place egg yolks, confectioners' sugar, rum, and vanilla in a medium-size bowl and whisk to blend well. Place bowl over boiling water to form a water bath. Do not let the bottom of the bowl touch the water. Whisk continuously until the mixture is the consistency of softly whipped cream, 4 to 5 minutes.

Remove from the heat and cool to the same temperature as the chocolate. Blend egg mixture and chocolate together with large strokes. Once chocolate is incorporated, gently fold the whipped cream into the chocolate mixture. Refrigerate until ready to use.

To assemble the dish, place mangoes in a large bowl and toss with Italian syrup. Then distribute the mangoes among 6 to 8 large wineglasses or colorful bowls. Top with the mousse, garnish with fresh mint, and serve cold.

◆▪ Pumpkin Bread Pudding ▪◆

Serves 12

■Although I like traditional pumpkin pie, everyone needs a change now and then. Try this new twist on an old favorite, whether it's for a holiday or just for a cozy night at home.

1 baguette, diced
1 cup toasted pecans
2½ cups half-and-half
¾ cup pumpkin purée
¾ cup plus ½ cup (optional) sugar
½ cup brown sugar
5 eggs
1 teaspoon pure vanilla extract
2 teaspoons ground cinnamon
1 teaspoon ground ginger
1 tablespoon crystallized ginger
½ teaspoon ground nutmeg
½ teaspoon ground allspice

Line a 10-inch springform pan with foil. Place diced bread and toasted pecans in foil-lined pan, mix, and set aside.

In a medium-size bowl, mix half-and-half, pumpkin, and ¾ cup sugar. Add brown sugar, eggs, vanilla, cinnamon, ground and crystallized ginger, nutmeg, and allspice. Pour over the bread and mix well. Let stand for about 20 minutes, while preheating oven to 350°. Mix again before placing in oven. Bake for 45 minutes, or until a knife inserted in the center comes out clean.

To serve, slice pudding into individual servings. Sprinkle each with about 2 teaspoons of sugar and caramelize the sugar with a propane torch. If you do not have a torch available, serve warm with softly whipped cream.

◆◆ Peach Gratin ◆◆

Serves 4

■ Just looking at this recipe makes me think of the warm, lazy days of summer. You don't have to use peaches; try a combination of fruit or berries. In the winter, you can serve the sabayon over Riesling Poached Pears. (Pictured opposite page 135.)

■ SABAYON

6 egg yolks
½ cup sugar
Zest of 1 orange
1 tablespoon orange juice concentrate
¼ cup dark rum
1 teaspoon chopped crystallized ginger
Pinch ground cinnamon

■ TO ASSEMBLE

1 tablespoon unsalted butter
6 or 7 large, ripe peaches

For the sabayon, in a metal bowl whisk together egg yolks, sugar, zest, orange juice concentrate, rum, ginger, and cinnamon. Place bowl over a simmering water bath. Make sure that the water does not touch the bottom of the bowl. Cook, whisking, until mixture is very thick and resembles softly whipped cream. Set aside.

To assemble, preheat broiler. Peel peaches and slice about ¼ inch thick. Lightly butter 4 ovenproof dessert plates. Arrange peach slices on plates. Spoon the sabayon on top of the peaches. Place under broiler for 3 to 4 minutes, or until golden brown. You may need to rotate the plates to ensure even browning. You can also use a propane torch to brown the tops. Serve warm, topped, if you like, with a small scoop of vanilla ice cream.

Ginger Pear Galette

Serves 6

■ I just love the way this dessert looks: sliced pears arranged in a circle, baked until golden brown, and then topped with a scoop of melting vanilla ice cream. The chopped ginger in the crust gives this dessert a tropical flavor. You can make this a day ahead and warm it just before serving. (Pictured opposite page 166.)

■ POACHED PEARS
6 large pears
6 cups pinot noir wine
1 cup sugar
1 stick cinnamon
1 tablespoon coarsely chopped gingerroot
Zest of 1 orange

■ CRUST
2⅓ cups flour
½ cup shortening
½ cup unsalted butter
1 teaspoon salt
2 teaspoons minced crystallized ginger
6 to 8 tablespoons cold water

■ TO ASSEMBLE
¼ cup unsalted butter, melted
½ cup sugar
1 pint good-quality vanilla ice cream

For the poached pears, peel the pears, cut in half, and set aside. In a large saucepan, bring wine, sugar, cinnamon, gingerroot, and zest to a boil. Add pears and cook over medium-high heat until fork-tender. If you have time, let the pears cool in the poaching liquid; if not, remove pears from liquid and, when cool enough to handle, slice about ¼ inch thick and set aside.

For the crust, place flour, shortening, butter, salt, and ginger in a medium-size bowl. With your fingertips, mix in the butter and shortening until the mixture resembles a coarse meal. Add enough water to moisten the dough and mix with a fork just until the dough comes together. Let the dough rest for 20 to 30 minutes.

To assemble, preheat oven to 375°. Roll dough out on a well-floured board to a thickness of about ¼ inch. Cut six 4- to 5-inch circles and place on a greased baking sheet. Brush each of the circles generously with some of the melted butter, using about half of it in all. Sprinkle with sugar, using about ¼ cup in all. Arrange the pear slices in a circle on each pastry circle. Brush each again with the remaining butter and sprinkle with the remaining sugar.

Bake until crust is golden brown, 30 to 40 minutes. Remove from oven and allow to cool for about 10 minutes. Remove from the pan and place on dessert plates. Top each with a scoop of ice cream and serve warm.

Raspberry Dessert Bruschetta

Serves 6

■ This is a twist on an item that people usually think of as an appetizer. With a sweeter bread and topping, it is a great light dessert. Try different berries or even peaches.

> ½ cup cream cheese
> 2 tablespoons half-and-half
> ¼ cup sugar
> Zest of 1 orange
> 2 tablespoons orange liqueur
> 2 tablespoons almond paste
> Pinch ground nutmeg
> Dash pure vanilla extract
> 6 slices Bistro Challah (page 30)
> 2 tablespoons unsalted butter
> 3 cups fresh raspberries
> ½ cup toasted almonds

In a food processor or mixer, place cream cheese, half-and-half, and sugar, and process to soften the cream cheese. Stop the machine and scrape down the sides. Run the machine a few more seconds, then stop and add zest, liqueur, almond paste, nutmeg, and vanilla. Process just until the mixture is thoroughly blended. Remove from the processor and set aside.

Butter one side of the challah slices and toast both sides on a grill or under the broiler. Allow toast to cool for a minute, then cut it in half on the diagonal.

Spread each toast with a generous amount of cream cheese mixture. Top each of the toasts with about ¼ cup berries. Sprinkle with toasted almonds and serve.

◆■ Almond Plum Strudel ■◆

Serves 8

■Instead of preparing traditional strudel dough, I've cut the preparation time by using phyllo dough. As with most of my recipes, you can vary the filling, but follow the method. Serve this strudel with ice cream.

■ **FILLING**
8 medium-size Italian plums or 5 large plums
½ cup almond paste
½ cup sugar
1 cup toasted, ground almonds
1 tablespoon cornstarch
½ teaspoon almond extract
Pinch ground ginger
Pinch ground nutmeg

■ **TO ASSEMBLE**
12 sheets phyllo dough
3 tablespoons unsalted butter, melted
2 tablespoons sugar

For the filling, slice plums into a large bowl and set aside. In a food processor or mixer bowl, place almond paste, sugar, almonds, cornstarch, almond extract, ginger, and nutmeg and process just until the mixture is thoroughly blended. Remove from the processor, mix with the sliced plums, and set aside.

To assemble the strudel, preheat oven to 350°. Lay 4 of the full sheets of phyllo out on a large piece of waxed paper and brush with some of the melted butter. Then sprinkle with some of the sugar. Repeat the process 2 more times. Spoon the filling down the center of the phyllo, leaving about 2 inches at each end. Fold the two short ends of the dough in toward the center. Then fold the long sides in to cover the center of the strudel. Flip over onto a greased baking sheet. Brush with butter and sprinkle with remaining sugar.

Bake for 30 to 40 minutes, or until the phyllo is golden brown. Let cool for about 10 minutes before slicing, then serve with cinnamon or vanilla ice cream.

◼◻ Pâte à Choux ◼◻
with Blackberries and Caramel Sauce

Serves 6

◼ Pâte à choux is the same pastry that is used for eclairs. I like it because it is so versatile. When berries are in season, I take full advantage with this dessert.

◼ PÂTE À CHOUX
1 cup water
½ cup unsalted butter, diced
1 tablespoon sugar
½ teaspoon salt
½ teaspoon pure vanilla extract
1 cup flour
4 large eggs

◼ CARAMEL SAUCE
1 cup sugar
¼ cup water
½ cup heavy cream
2 tablespoons unsalted butter

◼ TO ASSEMBLE
¾ cup heavy cream, whipped
1 tablespoon sugar
Dash pure vanilla extract
2 pints blackberries

For the pâte à choux, preheat oven to 425°. In a heavy saucepan, bring water, butter, sugar, salt, and vanilla to a boil. Add the flour all at once and stir over high heat until a dough forms and pulls away from the sides of the pan. Lower the heat and stir to dry the dough out a bit, about 3 minutes.

Remove from heat and add eggs, one at a time, stirring well or mixing with a mixer after each one. Before adding the last egg, check the consistency of the dough. It should be able to hold its shape without spreading out when piped onto a baking sheet. If the dough is still stiff, add the last egg.

Place dough in a piping bag fitted with a large star tip. On a greased baking sheet, pipe 6 large rosettes, about 2 inches in diameter. Bake until brown, 15 to 20 minutes. Reduce the oven temperature to 200° and cook for about 20 more minutes to dry out the pastries. Remove from the oven and cool.

For the caramel sauce, place sugar and water in a heavy saucepan and cook over high heat until the mixture starts to turn brown. Do not stir. Once the mixture has begun to brown, you may swirl the liquid to even out the color. Cook until mixture is a toasty brown, about another 2 minutes.

Add cream very carefully; it will boil up. Cook over high heat until mixture starts to thicken, about 5 minutes. Add butter and cook for about another 5 minutes to thicken it a bit more. When thick and shiny, remove from heat and keep warm or store in the refrigerator until ready to use.

To assemble the dish, whip heavy cream with sugar and vanilla extract until stiff peaks form; set aside. Cut pâte à choux in half and place a bottom half on each dessert place. Spoon the whipped cream inside the pastries, then top with blackberries. Place a pastry top on each, then drizzle with the warm caramel sauce. Serve immediately.

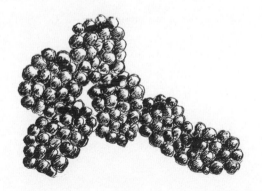

Pineapple Granita

Serves 4

■ The name "granita" comes from the shape of the ice crystals—large, flat and grainy instead of fine and creamy as in sorbet or sherbet. If you like, you can substitute pineapple juice for the wine, but if you do, add a bit more sugar to taste. You can also make granita with other fruit. It's a very refreshing way to finish a meal.

1 medium pineapple
1 cup sugar
2 cups riesling wine
1 teaspoon fresh lemon juice
Pinch ground nutmeg
Mint sprigs, for garnish

Peel, core, and dice the pineapple. Place in a blender with sugar, purée, and place in a medium-size metal bowl. Add wine, lemon juice, and nutmeg and mix well. Place the bowl in the freezer until mixture is about half frozen, 4 to 6 hours, depending on your freezer.

Scrape the granita with a large metal spoon. Return to the freezer and allow it to freeze solid, about 4 hours longer. Scrape again before serving. You want the ice to be in large, flat pieces or to resemble granite. Serve in cold wine goblets garnished with a sprig of fresh mint.

Meringue Shortcakes
with Blueberries

Serves 4

■ This is a lighter version of the classic shortcake. Try peaches or huckleberries instead of the blueberries. (Pictured opposite page 167.)

■ MERINGUE SHORTCAKES
6 egg whites
Pinch cream of tartar
1¼ cups sugar

■ BLUEBERRY FILLING
1 tablespoon unsalted butter
3 cups blueberries
½ cup sugar
¼ cup brandy
½ teaspoon ground cinnamon
¼ teaspoon ground nutmeg
¼ teaspoon ground ginger

■ TO ASSEMBLE
¾ cup heavy cream, whipped

For the meringues, preheat oven to 250°. Whip egg whites in a mixer bowl on high speed until foamy. Add cream of tartar and mix well. With the machine running, add sugar, about 1 tablespoon at a time. Once the sugar is incorporated, continue to mix until the egg whites are shiny and hold a stiff peak.

Place the meringue in a piping bag fitted with a large star tip. Line a baking sheet with parchment paper. Pipe eight 4-inch circles onto the parchment. If you like, you can draw circles on the paper to ensure they are even. Bake for about 1 hour, or until meringues are dry and crisp. Turn oven off and allow meringues to cool in oven. Remove from oven and set aside while you make the blueberry filling.

For the blueberry filling, heat butter in a large sauté pan until bubbling. Add blueberries and sauté until they start to soften, 2 to 3 minutes. Add sugar and brandy and cook until sugar is dissolved, about 2 minutes. Add cinnamon, nutmeg, and ginger and mix with berries. Remove from heat and allow to cool slightly.

To assemble, place one of the meringue layers on each of 4 plates. Top with about ⅓ cup of the blueberry filling, using about half of it in all. Add a bit of the whipped cream, then top with another meringue layer. Finish with more blueberry filling and then the last of the whipped cream. Serve immediately.

Riesling Poached Pears

■ This is a simple but elegant fall dessert that you can serve with Sabayon, vanilla flavored Crème Anglaise or ice cream. Or, if you are feeling really decadent, try chocolate ganache over the top of the pears.

> 4 cups riesling wine
> ¾ cups sugar
> Zest of 1 orange
> Dash pure vanilla extract
> 2 sticks cinnamon
> 6 pears, peeled and cored

Place the wine, sugar, zest, vanilla, and cinnamon in a large saucepan. Bring to a boil, add the pears, and lower the heat to a simmer. Cook the pears until tender, about 5 to 8 minutes. Remove from the heat and let cool slightly in the poaching liquid. Place each pear in an individual serving dish, spoon over some of the liquid, and serve warm topped with Crème Anglaise, ice cream, or Sabayon (see page 163).

MORNING FOOD

Hazelnut-Apple Pancakes

Makes about 1 dozen

■ I really don't like pancakes that are doughy and too thick, so I decided to come up with a recipe that was between a pancake and a crepe: not too light or too heavy. That means you can have a larger stack and not regret it later. Great with maple syrup or apple butter.

1¼ cups flour
⅓ cup toasted, finely ground hazelnuts
Pinch salt
2 teaspoons baking powder
½ teaspoon baking soda
1 egg
1⅓ cups buttermilk
2 tablespoons unsalted butter, melted
¼ cup applesauce
1 large Granny Smith apple, finely diced
½ teaspoon pure vanilla extract
1 tablespoon vegetable oil

Combine flour, nuts, salt, baking powder, and baking soda in a medium-size bowl. In a small bowl combine egg, buttermilk, butter, and applesauce. Fold into dry mixture. Do not overmix. Add apples and vanilla and stir just to combine.

Heat oil in a griddle or large sauté pan until hot. Ladle about ¼ cup of batter onto the hot griddle. Reduce the heat to medium and cook 1 or 2 minutes, or until golden brown. Flip and brown the other side. Serve warm with syrup or apple butter.

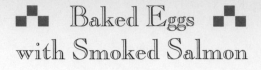

Baked Eggs
with Smoked Salmon

Serves 4

■ If you don't like smoked salmon, you can use smoked trout or sturgeon. Make this dish for brunch–maybe even for a special holiday brunch. Top with plain yogurt or sour cream if you like.

> 5 ounces hot-smoked salmon
> 2 teaspoons olive oil
> 3 cloves garlic, chopped
> 4 shallots, chopped
> 1 teaspoon chopped fresh thyme
> ½ teaspoon chopped fresh dill
> 9 eggs
> ½ cup half-and-half
> ½ cup grated Gouda cheese
> Salt and black pepper to taste

Preheat oven to 350°. Crumble smoked salmon and place in a large bowl. Heat oil in a small sauté pan until very hot. Add garlic and shallots and sauté until you can smell the aroma, about 2 minutes. Add thyme and dill; remove from heat.

In a medium-size bowl, whisk together eggs and half-and-half. Pour into the bowl with the smoked salmon. Add cooled garlic mixture and stir well. Pour into a well-greased 2-quart baking dish. Bake for about 20 minutes. Top with the Gouda cheese, salt, and pepper and bake 10 to 15 minutes more, or until a knife inserted in the center comes out clean. Serve hot topped with sour cream or yogurt, if desired.

Basil Breakfast Potatoes

Serves 4

■ Prepare these potatoes the night before then pop them in the oven the next morning. Try other fresh herbs such as thyme and oregano.

    5 medium potatoes, thinly sliced
    1 tablespoon olive oil
    3 cloves garlic, chopped
    2 shallots, chopped
    1 small onion, diced
    ½ cup dry sherry
    ½ cup grated Parmesan cheese
    2 tablespoons chopped fresh basil
    1 cup heavy cream
    Salt and cracked black pepper to taste

Preheat oven to 375°. Place the sliced potatoes in water to cover until needed. Heat oil in a medium sauté pan until very hot. Add garlic, shallots, and onions and sauté 2 to 3 minutes, until you can smell the aroma. Add sherry and boil over high heat to reduce until about ¼ cup of liquid remains. Remove from heat and allow to cool.

Lightly oil a 9 by 5-inch baking dish. Cover the bottom with about a third of the potatoes. Sprinkle with about a third of the onion mixture, then sprinkle with about a third of the cheese and the basil. Drizzle about ⅓ cup cream over the potato mixture and season lightly with salt and pepper. Top with another layer of potatoes and repeat the process. Top with one final layer of potatoes and repeat the process. Bake for about 40 minutes, or until the potatoes are fork-tender and the cheese is golden brown.

Ginger Orange Bread

Makes 1 loaf

■ This can be served for breakfast or for a very civilized afternoon tea. You can make a lot, freezing a few loaves for later cravings.

½ cup unsalted butter
¾ cup sugar
2 eggs
Zest of 1 orange
2 tablespoons orange juice concentrate
1½ cups flour
1½ teaspoons baking powder
¼ teaspoon baking soda
2 tablespoons diced crystallized ginger
1 cup ground walnuts

Preheat oven to 350°. In a large mixer bowl, cream butter and sugar until fluffy. Add eggs, one at a time, mixing well after each addition. Add zest and orange juice concentrate and mix.

In a small bowl, combine flour, baking powder, and baking soda. Mix well. Add flour mixture to butter mixture and mix. Add ginger and ground walnuts. Pour into a greased loaf pan and bake for about 1 hour, or until a knife inserted in the center comes out clean. Allow to cool before slicing.

Pecan Coffee Cake

Serves 12

■ I have this thing for coffee cake—I think there is just not enough of it served. When coffee cake is baking in my kitchen, I love to have a hot latte and a warm piece of cake just out of the oven.

■ CAKE
2 cups sugar
1 cup unsalted butter
2 eggs
2 cups flour
1 tablespoon baking powder
Pinch salt
1 cup sour cream
2 teaspoons pure vanilla extract

■ TOPPING
2 cups chopped pecans
3 tablespoons butter, softened
¼ cup brown sugar
¼ cup flour
1 teaspoon cinnamon
½ teaspoon ground ginger
½ teaspoon ground nutmeg
½ teaspoon ground allspice

For the cake, preheat oven to 350°. In a large mixer bowl, cream sugar and butter until fluffy. Add eggs, one at a time, mixing well after each addition.

In a small bowl, mix flour, baking powder, and salt. Add half the flour mixture to the butter mixture and mix. Add ½ cup sour cream and mix. Add remaining flour mixture and mix. Add remaining ½ cup sour cream and mix, then mix in vanilla.

Grease a 9 by 13-inch baking pan. Place batter in pan.

For the topping, in a small bowl mix pecans, butter, sugar, and flour to form a crumbly meal. Mix in cinnamon, ginger, nutmeg, and allspice. Sprinkle over top of cake. Bake for 45 to 60 minutes, until a knife inserted in the center comes out clean. Serve warm.

Corn Pudding

Serves 8

■ This dish is pretty substantial, so I like to serve it with muffins, fresh fruit, and some type of breakfast meat. You can use frozen corn, but it won't be as sweet and tender. Sometimes frozen corn is a bit chewy, and it may add extra water to the pudding.

2 teaspoons olive oil
1 small onion, diced
2 cloves garlic, chopped
4 cups fresh corn (about 10 ears)
3 eggs
½ cup flour
1 cup half-and-half
1 teaspoon chopped fresh basil
½ teaspoon cracked black pepper
Salt to taste
¼ cup grated Parmesan cheese
¼ cup grated Gouda cheese
½ cup grated sharp Cheddar cheese

Preheat oven to 350°. In a medium-size sauté pan, heat olive oil until very hot. Add onion and garlic and sauté until you can smell the aroma, 1 to 2 minutes. Add corn and sauté just to coat with the olive oil. Remove from heat and place in a large bowl to cool.

While corn is cooling, in a small bowl whisk together eggs, flour, half-and-half, basil, pepper, and salt until well blended. Pour over cooled corn and mix well.

Combine cheeses in a separate bowl. Pour corn mixture into a well-greased 9 by 9-inch baking dish, top with the cheeses, and bake for 35 to 45 minutes, or until top is golden brown and custard is set. Serve the pudding warm.

Poached Eggs
with Tarragon-Orange Hollandaise
Serves 4

■ This is not an everyday breakfast dish—serve it for a special occasion.

■TARRAGON-ORANGE HOLLANDAISE
1 cup white wine
½ cup tarragon vinegar
2 shallots, chopped
3 cloves garlic, chopped
1 tablespoon orange juice concentrate
Zest of 1 orange
2 teaspoons chopped fresh tarragon
4 egg yolks
1 cup unsalted butter, melted
Salt and black pepper to taste

■TO ASSEMBLE
1 tablespoon vinegar
4 slices toasted Bistro Challah (see page 30) or 4 croissants, split and toasted
8 slices pancetta, cooked until crisp
8 large eggs

For the hollandaise sauce, place wine, vinegar, shallots, garlic, orange juice concentrate, zest, and tarragon in a medium-size saucepan and boil over high heat to reduce until ½ cup of liquid remains, 5 to 8 minutes.

Place egg yolks in a medium-size metal bowl and whisk. Add a bit of the reduced liquid to the yolks to bring them to the same temperature. Stir the rest of the reduced liquid into the eggs. Place the bowl over a pan of boiling water; do not let the water touch the bottom of the bowl. Whisk egg mixture over the water bath until it is thick and resembles softly whipped cream. Remove bowl from heat and slowly whisk in butter. Season with salt and pepper. Keep warm but not hot.

To assemble, place about 2 inches of water in a large sauté pan. Add vinegar and bring to a boil. Meanwhile, cut bread in half on the diagonal and place on a baking sheet. Lay pancetta on top of toast and set aside. When water comes to a boil, lower to simmering. Break the eggs into a bowl and gently place them in the water. Cook just until eggs are set, about 3 minutes. With a slotted spoon, remove the eggs from the water and allow them to drain. Place an egg on top of each piece of toast then top with some hollandaise. Serve warm.

Prosciutto Breakfast Strata

Serves 6

■ The method for this breakfast dish may sound a bit time-consuming, but the good news is that most of it is done the day before. That's something I really like, since I am not a morning person. If you want, you can substitute cooked sausage for the prosciutto, or even omit the meat entirely and make it vegetarian. (Pictured opposite.)

1½ cups milk
¾ cup dry white wine
1 loaf French bread, sliced ½ inch thick
8 ounces prosciutto, julienned
1 cup fresh basil leaves
1½ cups soft, fresh goat cheese
⅓ cup sun-dried tomatoes, julienned
3 red bell peppers, roasted, peeled, seeded, and julienned (see page 200)
4 eggs
2 cloves garlic, chopped
½ cup heavy cream
Salt and black pepper to taste

In a medium-size bowl, mix together milk and white wine. Dip the bread in the milk mixture, but do not soak the bread.

Grease a 12-inch baking dish. Place a layer of bread on the bottom of the baking dish. Place one third of the prosciutto on top of the bread, followed by one third of the basil leaves. Over the top crumble one third of the goat cheese, then place one third of the sun-dried tomatoes and one third of the roasted peppers overall. Repeat entire layering process, from bread to peppers, twice more until the pan is full.

In a medium-size bowl, mix together eggs, garlic, cream, salt, and pepper. Pour over the strata and place in the refrigerator overnight.

The next morning, remove the strata from the refrigerator and let come to room temperature while you preheat the oven to 350°. Bake the strata for 45 to 50 minutes, or until golden brown. Serve hot.

Spiced Pecan French Toast

Serves 6

■ We serve this French toast at the bistro. We make the custard the night before, then soak the bread in the morning before cooking the toast. If you don't like pecans, you can substitute hazelnuts or walnuts. Serve it with fresh, seasonal fruit. (Pictured opposite.)

5 eggs
1½ cups half-and-half
½ cup toasted, ground pecans
2 tablespoons sugar
½ teaspoon pure vanilla extract
2 teaspoons ground cinnamon
½ teaspoon ground nutmeg
½ teaspoon ground ginger
½ teaspoon ground allspice
Zest of 1 orange
12 slices French bread (if bread is small, use 18 slices)
6 tablespoons unsalted butter
Maple syrup and butter, as an accompaniment

In a large bowl, combine eggs, half-and-half, pecans, and sugar and mix well. Add vanilla, cinnamon, nutmeg, ginger, allspice, and orange zest and mix well. Soak bread in this mixture for about 10 minutes.

Heat about 2 tablespoons of the butter in a large sauté pan and place about one third of the slices in the pan (they should fit in one layer). Cook for 3 to 4 minutes per side, or until golden brown. Remove from pan and keep in a warm oven while you cook the rest of the toast. Add more butter to pan before cooking another batch. Serve warm with maple syrup and butter.

■■ Sausage Scramble in Flour Tortillas ■■
with Tomatillo Salsa

Serves 4

■ When you make this dish you can fill the tortillas with the eggs any way you want—form a cone with the tortilla or roll it like a burrito. You can substitute fresh vegetables, like tomatoes or sautéed peppers, for the sausage.

■ TOMATILLO SALSA
8 tomatillos, husks removed
3 cloves garlic
1 small red onion, minced
1 jalapeño, diced
Juice of 1 lime
3 tablespoons vegetable oil
1 teaspoon ground cumin
½ teaspoon ground coriander
1 teaspoon chopped cilantro
Salt and black pepper to taste

■ SAUSAGE SCRAMBLE
4 large flour tortillas
8 ounces chorizo sausage
10 eggs
¼ cup water
½ teaspoon chile powder
Salt and black pepper to taste
⅓ cup sour cream
⅓ cup grated sharp Cheddar cheese

For the salsa, preheat oven to 425°. Place tomatillos in a roasting pan and roast for about 20 minutes. Remove from oven and allow to cool for about 10 minutes. Place in food processor with garlic and process until smooth.

Pour into a medium-size bowl and add onion, jalapeño, lime juice, oil, cumin, coriander, and cilantro; mix well. Season with salt and pepper. Set aside until ready to use.

For the scramble, cover the tortillas with a damp towel and place in a warm oven to warm while you cook the eggs. Crumble chorizo into a medium-size sauté pan and sauté until the sausage is just cooked through. In a large bowl, whisk together eggs, water, chile powder, salt, and pepper and mix well. Pour all but 2 teaspoons of the fat from the sauté pan, then add the egg mixture to the sausage and cook, stirring, just until set, 3 to 4 minutes. Spoon the eggs onto the middle of the warm tortillas. Fold the ends of the tortillas over, then roll up like an egg roll. Top with tomatillo salsa, sour cream, and Cheddar cheese. Serve warm.

Orange-Scented Waffles
with Blueberry Compote

Serves 6

■ I know you probably haven't made homemade waffles in years, but these are reserved for lazy Saturday or Sunday mornings. My three-year-old daughter Savannah loves to help whip up the egg whites, which really makes it fun.

■ **BLUEBERRY COMPOTE**
1 tablespoon unsalted butter
3 pints blueberries
½ cup sugar
¼ cup fresh orange juice
¼ cup orange liqueur

■ **ORANGE-SCENTED WAFFLES**
2 cups flour
¼ teaspoon baking soda
Pinch salt
1 tablespoon sugar
1 tablespoon orange juice concentrate
1¾ cups milk
¼ cup club soda or 7-Up
4 large eggs, separated
¼ cup unsalted butter, melted
Zest of 1 orange

For the compote, heat butter in a large sauté pan until it starts to bubble. Add blueberries and sauté for 2 minutes just to soften the berries. Add sugar, orange juice, and liqueur and bring the mixture to a boil. Reduce heat to medium low and simmer for 5 minutes, just until the mixture is thick and syrupy. Keep warm while you make the waffles.

For the waffles, heat a waffle iron. Place flour, baking soda, salt, and sugar in a medium-size bowl and mix well. In another bowl, mix together orange juice concentrate, milk, club soda, egg yolks, butter, and orange zest. Pour egg mixture into the flour mixture and stir just until batter comes together.

Using an electric mixer, beat egg whites just until soft peaks form. Fold egg whites into batter, using large gestures. Spoon some of the batter into a hot, well-greased waffle iron. Cook until the waffle is golden brown. Repeat with remaining batter. Serve warm with blueberry compote. If you really want to be decadent, top with whipped cream.

Roasted Vegetable Hash
with Poached Eggs

Serves 6

■ Here's another classical dish that I do a bit differently. This is a vegetarian version of the classic breakfast dish. You can make the hash the night before and heat it up in the morning while poaching the eggs. Have hot sauce on hand to serve as an accompaniment.

■ HASH

1 tablespoon olive oil
4 potatoes, diced
1 sweet potato, diced
1 onion, diced
3 cloves garlic, chopped
2 zucchini, diced
1 yellow squash, diced
2 tomatoes, seeded and diced
2 dashes Worcestershire sauce
2 tablespoons cayenne sauce
¼ cup chopped fresh basil
Salt and black pepper to taste

■ POACHED EGGS

6 cups water
1 tablespoon white wine vinegar
12 eggs

For the hash, heat olive oil in a very large sauté pan until very hot. Add potatoes and sweet potatoes and cook until well browned, 4 to 5 minutes. Add onion and garlic and sauté until you can smell the aroma. Add zucchini and yellow squash and sauté until crisp-tender, 3 to 4 minutes. Add tomatoes and toss with the vegetables. Season the mixture with Worcestershire sauce, cayenne sauce, basil, salt, and pepper and toss well. Keep warm while poaching the eggs.

To poach the eggs, heat water and vinegar until simmering in a large sauté pan with sides. Break the eggs into a cup and gently add them into the water. Poach for 4 to 5 minutes, or until yolk is nearly cooked. Remove eggs from pan with a slotted spoon to drain the liquid.

Divide the hash among 6 plates, then top each serving with 2 poached eggs. Serve warm, with hot sauce on the side.

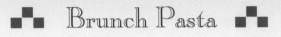

Brunch Pasta

Serves 6

■ When you're having a noon brunch, pasta is quite appropriate. The bacon in this makes it more breakfastlike, and the vegetables and a sauce made with chicken stock round out this dish.

1 tablespoon olive oil
1 medium onion, diced
3 cloves garlic, chopped
8 slices bacon, diced
12 spears asparagus, blanched and sliced on an angle
½ cup fresh, shelled peas
½ cup Chicken Stock (see page 196)
1½ pounds fresh pasta, cooked al dente
¾ cup grated Parmesan cheese
Salt and black pepper to taste

Heat olive oil in a large sauté pan until very hot. Add onion and garlic and sauté until you can smell the aroma. Add the diced bacon and cook over low to medium heat until bacon is crisp. Add asparagus and peas and toss with the bacon.

Add chicken stock and boil over high heat for 2 minutes to reduce. Add pasta and cook until the pasta is heated through. Add all but ⅓ cup of the Parmesan cheese to the pasta and toss well. Season with salt and pepper. Place on a platter and top with the rest of the Parmesan cheese. Serve hot.

Mashed Potato Cakes

Serves 4

■ These are like pancakes made with mashed potatoes. You can use leftover mashed potatoes if you happen to have some around. Serve these for breakfast or as a side dish at lunch or dinner.

4 large potatoes, peeled and diced
4 cloves garlic
½ teaspoon chopped fresh thyme
½ teaspoon chopped fresh marjoram
½ teaspoon chopped fresh oregano
½ teaspoon cracked black pepper
Salt to taste
½ cup flour
2 tablespoons olive oil

Place potatoes and whole garlic cloves in a medium-size saucepan and add water to cover. Place on high heat and boil until the potatoes are tender.

Strain off the water, then mash the potatoes and garlic. Add thyme, marjoram, oregano, pepper, and salt.

Form mixture into 8 patties. Dredge the patties in flour to coat them and then dust them off.

Heat 1 tablespoon of the olive oil in a large sauté pan until very hot. Place 4 of the patties in the pan and brown well on each side, 2 to 3 minutes per side. Keep warm while you cook the rest of the patties in the remaining olive oil. Serve the patties warm.

Poached Pears
Broiled with Brown Sugar

Serves 6

■ I came up with the idea for this dish when I was thinking about traditional items served at breakfast. We broil grapefruit; why not try broiling some other type of fruit? Pears, with their great texture, proved to be the perfect choice.

6 cups riesling wine or other sweet white wine
1 cup sugar
Zest of 1 orange
Dash pure vanilla extract
2 cinnamon sticks
2 whole cloves
3 pears, peeled and cut in half
½ cup brown sugar
1 cup Crème Fraîche (see page 141)
½ cup confectioners' sugar

To poach the pears, place wine, sugar, orange zest, vanilla, cinnamon, and cloves in a heavy, medium-size saucepan and bring to a boil over high heat. Add pears, reduce heat to medium, and simmer until they are fork-tender. Cool in the liquid until you can handle the pears.

Preheat broiler. Remove pears from liquid and cut into ¼-inch-thick slices. Arrange about half a pear on each of 6 ovenproof plates. Sprinkle pears generously with brown sugar. Place plates under broiler and broil until the brown sugar is melted and bubbling.

While the pears are broiling, mix together crème fraîche and confectioners' sugar. Remove pears carefully from oven, drizzle with crème fraîche, and serve warm.

Fruit Salad
with Honey Yogurt Dressing

Serves 6

■ I like to have fruit of some kind with breakfast or brunch, but sliced fruit or a fruit plate is boring. Why not serve a refreshing fruit salad instead? Use a nonfat yogurt in the dressing, if you like, to make this a low-fat dish.

■ **HONEY YOGURT DRESSING**
1½ cups plain yogurt
¼ cup confectioners' sugar
⅓ cup honey
Dash almond extract
½ teaspoon ground ginger
½ teaspoon ground allspice
Pinch ground cinnamon
1 teaspoon chopped fresh mint

■ **FRUIT SALAD**
1 pint strawberries, hulled and quartered
1 small cantaloupe, peeled and diced
1 small pineapple, peeled and diced
1 pint blueberries
2 mangoes, peeled and diced
2 papayas, peeled and diced
½ cup toasted almonds

For the dressing, combine yogurt, confectioners' sugar, and honey in a bowl, mixing well. Add almond extract, ginger, allspice, cinnamon, and mint and mix well. Set aside while you prepare the fruit.

For the salad, place the fruit in a bowl and toss to mix. Add dressing and mix well. Place in refrigerator until ready to serve. Top with toasted almonds just before serving.

Breakfast Fruit Crisp

Serves 12

■ You have a choice with this dish: you can serve it as a fruit course, or you can save it for dessert. Use any berries or fruits that are in season. This is a nice dessert to serve after the Brunch Pasta.

■ TOPPING
1 cup flour
1 cup granola
½ cup toasted hazelnuts or pecans
¼ cup coconut
½ teaspoon pure vanilla extract
½ cup brown sugar
1 cup unsalted butter

■ FILLING
2 pints raspberries or blackberries
2 pints strawberries, hulled and quartered
1 cup sugar
Pinch ground cinnamon
½ teaspoon ground allspice
½ teaspoon ground nutmeg
½ teaspoon pure vanilla extract

■ GARNISH
2 cups vanilla yogurt
Fresh mint

Preheat oven to 350°. For the topping, place flour, granola, nuts, coconut, vanilla, and brown sugar in a medium-size bowl and mix well. Add the butter and mix with your fingertips until the mixture resembles a coarse dough. Set aside.

For the filling, place berries, sugar, cinnamon, allspice, nutmeg, and vanilla in a large bowl and toss to mix. Place in a 9 by 11-inch baking dish. Crumble topping over berry mixture.

Bake for 30 to 40 minutes, or until topping is golden brown. Remove from oven and allow to cool slightly.

To serve, place the warm crisp on plates and top with yogurt and mint.

BASICS

Smoked Chicken

Serves 6

■ Smoking chicken takes a bit longer than smoking tomatoes, but it is still very simple. You can use smoked chicken for sandwiches or in pasta. The brine/marinade must be prepared a day in advance.

1½ cups dry red wine
½ cup apple cider
½ cup brown sugar
¼ cup kosher salt
½ teaspoon peppercorns
1 stick cinnamon
3 sprigs thyme
6 boneless chicken breasts, 6 ounces each

In a medium-sized saucepan, combine the wine, cider, sugar, salt, peppercorns, cinnamon, and thyme, and bring to a boil over high heat. Remove from the heat and cool until chilled. In a large bowl, pour brine over chicken breasts, cover, and marinate for 24 hours.

Prepare the coals by piling briquettes on one side of the barbecue, lighting them, and allowing them to burn down until gray. Meanwhile, remove chicken from the brine and allow to drain well.

Remove grill from barbecue. Place smoking chips (alder, apple, grape vine, tea, or any type of hardwood) on the coals and put grill back on barbecue. Place chicken on the other side of the grill from the coals. Cover barbecue, and let smoke for about 2 hours, adding more chips if the smoke dies out. Remove chicken from the heat, cover, and place in the refrigerator. Chill completely before using, about 1 to 2 hours.

Chicken or Turkey Stock

Makes about 4 cups

2 pounds chicken or turkey bones, rinsed
2 onions, coarsely chopped
2 carrots, coarsely chopped
2 stalks celery, coarsely chooped
3 cloves garlic, chopped
4 sprigs thyme
8 cups water
1 bay leaf

In a large stockpot over high heat, bring the bones, onions, carrots, celery, garlic, thyme, and water just to a boil. Add the bay leaf. Reduce the heat and simmer for 4 to 6 hours, or until the stock is richly flavored. Strain through a fine sieve into a bowl and use immediately, or allow to cool to room temperature before refrigerating.

This stock keeps in the refrigerator for up to one week and can be frozen.

Beef, Veal, or Lamb Stock

Makes about 4 cups

5 pounds beef, veal, or lamb bones
2 onions, coarsely chopped
1 carrot, coarsely chopped
3 stalks celery, coarsely chopped
3 cloves garlic, chopped
2 tablespoons tomato paste
1 cup dry red wine
8 cups water
1 bay leaf

Preheat the oven to 450°.

In a roasting pan, place the bones, onions, carrot, celery, and garlic and roast for about 1 hour, or until the bones turn golden brown. Spread the tomato paste over the mixture and roast for 10 more minutes.

Transfer the mixture to a large stockpot. Add the wine to the roasting pan and, using a wooden spoon, scrape up all the brown bits from the bottom of the pan. Pour this liquid into the stockpot. Add the water and bay leaf. Bring to a boil over high heat. Reduce the heat and simmer for 6 to 8 hours, until the stock is full of flavor. Strain through a fine sieve into a bowl and use immediately, or allow to cool to room temperature before refrigerating.

This stock keeps in the refrigerator for up to one week and can be frozen.

Fish Stock

Makes about 4 cups

½ pound fish bones (use bones from white fish only)
2 leeks
1 tablespoon unsalted butter
2 large onions, coarsely chopped
2 stalks celery, coarsely chopped
3 cloves garlic, chopped
¼ cup mushroom stems
1 cup dry white wine
4 sprigs thyme
8 cups water

Coarsely chop the fish bones and place them in a large bowl or stockpot. Cover with cold water and soak for 1 or 2 hours to remove any remaining traces of blood.

Discard the green portion of the leeks. Trim and rinse the whites thoroughly, then coarsely chop. In a large stockpot over high temperature, heat the butter until bubbling. Add the leeks, onions, celery, garlic, and mushroom stems and sauté until they begin to give off their aroma, 3 or 4 minutes. Add the wine and bones, reduce heat, and sweat the mixture, covered, for about 8 minutes. Add the thyme and water and simmer, uncovered, for 25 minutes more. Strain through a fine sieve into a bowl and use immediately, or allow to cool to room temperature before refrigerating.

This stock keeps in the refrigerator for up to one week and can be frozen.

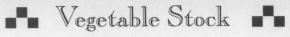

Vegetable Stock

Makes about 4 cups

3 onions, coarsely chopped
4 carrots, coarsely chopped
5 stalks celery, coarsely chopped
4 ounces mushrooms, coarsely chopped
4 cloves garlic, chopped
3 shallots, chopped
6 sprigs thyme
8 cups water

In a large stockpot over high heat, bring the onions, carrots, celery, mushrooms, garlic, shallots, thyme, and water just to a boil. Reduce the heat and simmer for about 1 hour, or until the stock is richly flavored. Strain through a fine sieve into a bowl and use immediately, or allow to cool to room temperature before refrigerating.

This stock keeps in the refrigerator for up to one week and can be frozen.

Roasted Garlic

■For a tasty appetizer, spread this garlic on bread and serve with mustard and goat cheese.

1 head garlic
2 tablespoons olive oil

Preheat the oven to 250°.

Slice about ¼ inch off the top of the garlic head and discard. Place the head in a small baking dish or ovenproof sauté pan. Drizzle the oil over it. Roast until soft, 40 to 50 minutes.

Roasted Garlic will keep in the refrigerator for 2 or 3 weeks.

◼◆ Roasted Shallots ◼◆

◼Roasted shallots are also wonderful with steaks and grilled chicken.

> 6 shallots, peeled
> ¼ cup olive oil

Preheat the oven to 250°.

Place the shallots and olive oil in a small baking dish or ovenproof sauté pan and roast until soft, about 40 minutes.

Roasted Shallots will keep in the refrigerator for up to 2 weeks.

◆◼ Sun-Dried Tomato Tapenade ◼◆

Serves 4

◼At the restaurant, we serve crostini topped with softened Gorgonzola and this tapenade, drizzled with a bit of extra-virgin olive oil. A couple of crostini and a salad make a light lunch or dinner.

> 1 cup chopped sun-dried tomatoes
> 2 cloves garlic
> ½ teaspoon tomato paste
> 1 teaspoon capers
> ⅓ cup extra-virgin olive oil
> Salt and black pepper to taste

Place tomatoes, garlic, tomato paste, and capers in a food processor and blend until smooth. With the machine running, add olive oil and process until well blended. Season with salt and pepper.

You can either serve this in a bowl with crostini (toast) on the side, or spread it on toast triangles and crumble Gorgonzola cheese on top.

Roasted Peppers

■ Add roasted peppers to pastas, soups, or salads. Roasted bell peppers are also good just by themselves.

Red bell peppers, or chiles

Preheat the broiler. Place the peppers on a baking sheet or in a shallow ovenproof dish and broil until the skins blister and turn brown. Turn the peppers until charred on all sides, about 15 minutes. Transfer the roasted peppers to a bowl, cover with plastic wrap, and set aside to cool.

When the peppers are cool enough to handle, peel the skins and remove stems and seeds. Use immediately or drizzle with olive oil and store in the refrigerator for up to 2 months.

Roasted Pepper Salsa

Makes about 1 cup

■ Salsa can be made with a huge variety of fruits and vegetables—the only basic requirement of salsa is that it be zesty and lively. Take this basic recipe and build on it to create your own salsa.

3 red bell peppers, roasted, peeled, and diced (see above)
3 cloves garlic, chopped
¼ cup tomato purée
1 small red onion, diced
¼ cup chopped fresh basil
2 tablespoons red wine vinegar
3 tablespoons olive oil
2 Anaheim chiles, roasted, peeled, and diced (see above)
½ teaspoon dried coriander
½ teaspoon chile powder
Salt and pepper to taste

In a large bowl, toss together the bell peppers, garlic, tomato purée, red onion, and basil. Add vinegar, olive oil, and chiles, and mix well. Season with coriander, chile powder, salt, and pepper. Let stand for about 30 minutes before serving.

Roasted Red Pepper Sauce

Makes 1¾ cups

■ This is a simple sauce to serve with crab cakes. Use a blender when making so that the sauce will emulsify better and have a creamier texture. You can make this up to a week ahead of time.

> Juice of 1 lemon
> 1 tablespoon Dijon-style mustard
> ¼ cup white wine vinegar
> 2 anchovy fillets
> 2 cloves garlic
> 1½ cups olive oil
> 1 red bell pepper, roasted, peeled, and seeded (see page 200)
> Salt and black pepper to taste

Place lemon juice, mustard, vinegar, anchovies, and garlic in a blender. Purée. With the motor running, slowly drizzle in the olive oil. Once all the oil is incorporated, add roasted pepper and purée until smooth. Season with salt and pepper. Serve with crab cakes.

Smoked Tomatoes

Smoking tomatoes gives them a rich quality that makes both sauces and soups taste terrific. It is an easy process that can be done up to 5 days ahead of when you want to use the tomatoes—store in a covered plastic container in the refrigerator. Use large, vine-ripened tomatoes.

Prepare the coals by piling briquettes on one side of the barbecue and lighting them. Let them burn until they are gray in color. Meanwhile, core and slice about 12 tomatoes in half horizontally, then seed in a small bowl of water. Remove grill from barbecue and spray with an oil spray. Place smoking chips (alder, apple, grape vines, tea, or any type of hardwood) on the coals, and put grill back on barbecue. Place tomatoes flat side down on the opposite side of the grill from the coals. Cover barbecue, and let smoke for 1 to 2 hours, adding more chips if the smoke dies down. Tomatoes should be nicely browned and have a lightly smoky smell.

Quick Puff Pastry

Makes 2 pounds

■ This is the fast version of classic puff pastry. Make a double batch and keep blocks of the pastry frozen for when you want to create a quick dessert or appetizer.

> 4½ cups flour
> 2 cups (1 pound) unsalted butter, diced
> 1 teaspoon salt
> 1 cup plus 2 tablespoons cold water

Place flour, diced butter, and salt in a large mixing bowl. With your fingertips, mix the butter into the flour to make a coarse meal. It's all right if you still have some large pieces of butter. Pour in about 1 cup of water, just enough to moisten the dough. Mix the dough with a fork just to moisten.

Pour dough onto a floured board. Form into a rough rectangle. Fold over one third of the dough toward the center. Fold the other third over toward the center. Turn the dough 90 degrees. Sprinkle with flour and roll out into a rectangle about 20 by 6 inches. Fold the dough by thirds again. Again rotate 90 degrees, flour, and roll out. Repeat the process two more times.

Chill the dough for at least 1 hour before rolling out. You may also freeze the dough. Cut it into smaller pieces before freezing.

Orange–White Chocolate Sauce

Makes ¾ cup

■ This can be used as a sauce for Poached Ginger Cheesecake or just over vanilla ice cream. It is best served slightly warm.

> 6 ounces white chocolate
> ½ cup heavy cream
> 2 tablespoons orange juice concentrate
> 1 tablespoon finely chopped gingerroot

Place chocolate, cream, orange juice concentrate, and gingerroot in a metal bowl. Place over simmering water until about half the chocolate is melted. Remove from the heat, keeping the bowl over the water bath. Let chocolate melt the rest of the way. Mix with a whisk. If the sauce is too thick, you can thin it with a bit of half-and-half. Serve warm over your favorite dessert or ice cream.

Crème Anglaise

Makes 1 ¼ cups

■ This is a very classical dessert sauce. You can flavor the basic Crème Anglaise with any kind of liqueur or berry purée.

> 1 cup half-and-half
> ½ cup sugar
> 1 vanilla bean, split
> 4 egg yolks
> 2 tablespoons unsalted butter

Combine half-and-half, ¼ cup of the sugar, and the split vanilla bean in a medium-size saucepan over medium heat. Place egg yolks in a bowl and whisk in the remaining ¼ cup sugar. When the half-and-half mixture just comes to a boil, remove from heat and stir a bit into the egg yolk mixture to temper it. Then add the egg yolk mixture to the half-and-half mixture. Return to the stove and cook the sauce over medium heat until it is thick enough to coat a spoon. Stir in butter and serve warm or cold.

Port Sauce

■ This sauce is should be light but flavorful. You can easily double the recipe if you are serving this for a large group. Serve over roast turkey.

> 1 tablespoon olive oil
> 2 cloves garlic, chopped
> 3 shallots, chopped
> 1 cup port wine
> 3 cups Chicken or Turkey Stock (see page 196)
> ¼ cup dried cherries
> 1 tablespoon chopped fresh thyme
> 1 teaspoon cracked black pepper
> Salt to taste

In a medium-size saucepan, heat olive oil until very hot. Add garlic and shallots and sauté until you can smell the aroma. Add port and boil to reduce until about ½ cup remain. Add stock and reduce again until about 1½ cups of liquid remain. Add thyme, black pepper, and salt. Serve hot.

◼︎◻︎ Homemade Herb Mustard ◻︎◼︎

Makes 2 cups

◼ This is a very easy recipe and once you make a batch you can keep it for months. It is also a wonderful gift around the holidays.

        ½ cup mustard seeds
        2 tablespoons dry mustard
        ¾ cup water
        ¾ cup white wine vinegar or herb vinegar
        1 tablespoon honey
        2 tablespoons sugar
        2 teaspoons salt
        1½ teaspoons black pepper
        1 tablespoon chopped fresh basil
        1 tablespoon chopped fresh thyme
        1 teaspoon chopped fresh rosemary
        1 teaspoon chopped fresh sage

Place mustard seeds and dry mustard in a spice grinder or blender and blend to break the seeds up. I prefer a coarse grind to give the mustard some texture. Place the ground mustard seed and dry mustard in a bowl and pour the water over the top. Stir and cover. Let the mixture stand for 4 to 5 hours, stirring once or twice.

Put the mixture in a food processor and add vinegar, honey, sugar, salt, pepper, basil, thyme, rosemary, and sage. Purée until smooth. If mustard seems too dry, add warm water to make a smooth paste. Store in a jar at room temperature until the mustard mellows to your taste, up to 2 weeks for a very mellow mustard.

Simple Butter Sauce

Makes 1 cup

■ Once you can make one butter sauce you can make sauce of any flavor you can dream of. It's wonderful plain with Steamed Salmon with Sautéed Spinach and Hazelnuts.

>1 cup dry white wine
>¼ cup white wine vinegar
>2 tablespoons lemon juice
>2 cloves garlic, chopped
>2 shallots, chopped
>1 cup unsalted butter
>Salt and black pepper to taste

In a medium-size saucepan, combine the wine, vinegar, lemon juice, garlic, and shallots. Boil over high heat to reduce the liquid until about ¼ cup remains. Slowly whisk in the butter, making sure that you keep the temperature even, not too hot or too cold. Once all the butter has been added and you have a smooth, creamy sauce, season with salt and pepper. Serve. Do not try to hold the sauce longer than 1 hour.

Basil Pesto

Makes 2 cups

■ Pesto is a staple for any good chef's repertoire; you can use this easy pesto as anything from a pasta sauce to a sandwich spread.

>2 cups basil leaves
>4 cloves garlic
>1 cup pine nuts or walnuts
>¾ cup grated Parmesan cheese
>¾ cup extra-virgin olive oil

Place basil, garlic, nuts, and Parmesan cheese in a food processor and process until mixture forms a paste. Stop the machine and scrape down the sides. With the machine running, add the olive oil until all the oil is incorporated. Store in the refrigerator until ready to use, up to a week.

Tarragon Pesto

Makes ½ cup

■ You can use this as you would a basil pesto. My favorite way to use it is to cut slits into a salmon fillet and pipe the pesto into the pockets, then bake it for about 10 minutes. It's beautiful, and it tastes unbelievable.

1 bunch tarragon (½ cup)
½ bunch spinach, stems trimmed
3 cloves garlic, coarsely chopped
Zest of 1 lemon
¼ cup grated Parmesan cheese
¼ cup coarsely chopped walnuts
⅓ cup olive oil
Pinch cracked black pepper

Place tarragon leaves, spinach, garlic, and lemon zest in a food processor and process to chop. When the mixture is chopped very fine, add cheese and walnuts and process to chop the walnuts. With the motor running, add the olive oil and black pepper. Process until you have a smooth paste. Remove from processor and refrigerate until ready to use.

British Terms

NORTH AMERICAN TERM	BRITISH TERM	NORTH AMERICAN TERM	BRITISH TERM
arugula	rocket	halibut	jewfish
baking sheet	baking tray	heavy cream	double cream
baking soda	bicarbonate of soda	Italian parsley	flat-leaf parsley
Belgian endive	use chicory	New York steak	sirloin or rump steak
bell pepper	capsicum/ sweet pepper	papaya	pawpaw
cantaloupe	rockmelon	rack of lamb	crown roast
chops	cutlets	pitted	stoned/seeded
cilantro	fresh coriander	red onion	Spanish onion
cod	bluefish	romaine lettuce	Cos lettuce
confectioners' sugar	icing sugar	shrimp	prawn(s)
cookies	biscuits	snow peas	mange tout
cornmeal	cornmeal flour	sour cream	substitute crème fraîche
eggplant	aubergine(s)		
Granny Smith apple	cooking apple	spinach	English spinach
green onion	spring onion	tomato paste	tomato purée
ground	minced	vanilla extract	vanilla essence
half-and-half	half milk, half cream	zucchini	courgette(s)

Conversion Charts

■ VOLUME

formulas:
1 teaspoon = 4.93 mL
1 tablespoon = 14.79 mL/3 teaspoons
1 cup = 236.59 mL/16 tablespoons
1 L = 202.88 teaspoons/67.63 tablespoons/
    4.23 cups

1 teaspoon	5 mL
½ tablespoon	7 mL
2 teaspoons	10 mL
1 tablespoon (3 teaspoons)	15 mL
4 teaspoons	20 mL
1 ½ tablespoons	22 mL
5 teaspoons	25 mL
2 tablespoons (6 teaspoons)	30 mL
3 tablespoons	44 mL
¼ cup (4 tablespoons)	59 mL
⅓ cup	78 mL
½ cup (8 tablespoons)	118 mL
⅔ cup	159 mL
¾ cup (12 tablespoons)	177 mL
1 cup	237 mL
2 cups	473 mL
3 cups	710 mL
1 quart (4 cups)	946 mL
5 cups	1.2 L
6 cups	1.4 L
7 cups	1.7 L
2 quarts (8 cups)	1.9 L

■ LENGTH

formulas:
1 inch = 2.54 cm
1 foot = .3 m/12 inches
1 cm = .39 inch
1 m = 3.28 feet/39.37 inches

¼ inch	.6 cm
½ inch	1 cm
¾ inch	2 cm
1 inch	2.5 cm
1 ½ inches	4 cm
2 inches	5 cm
2 ½ inches	6 cm
3 inches	8 cm
3 ½ inches	9 cm
4 inches	10 cm
5 inches	13 cm
6 inches (½ foot)	15 cm
7 inches	18 cm
8 inches	20 cm
9 inches	23 cm
10 inches	25 cm
11 inches	28 cm
12 inches (1 foot)	30 cm
18 inches (1 and ½ foot)	46 cm

■ WEIGHT

1 ounce = 28.35 g
1 pound = 453.59 g/16 ounces
1 kg = 2.2 pounds

½ ounce	14 g
1 ounce	28 g
2 ounces	57 g
3 ounces	85 g
4 ounces (¼ pound)	113 g
5 ounces	142 g
6 ounces	170 g
7 ounces	198 g
8 ounces (½ pound)	227 g
9 ounces	255 g
10 ounces	283 g
11 ounces	312 g
12 ounces	340 g
13 ounces	369 g
14 ounces	397 g
15 ounces	425 g
1 pound (16 ounces)	454 g
2 pounds	907 g
3 pounds	1.4 kg
4 pounds	1.8 kg
4 ½ pounds	2 kg

■ TEMPERATURE

formulas:
$9/5\ C + 32 = F$
$(F - 32) \times 5/9 = C$

275°F	135°C/gas mark 1
300°F	149°C/gas mark 2
325°F	163°C/gas mark 3
350°F	177°C/gas mark 4
375°F	191°C/gas mark 5
400°F	204°C/gas mark 6
425°F	218°C/gas mark 7
450°F	232°C/gas mark 8
475°F	246°C/gas mark 9
500°F	260°C

Index

Italics refer to menu suggestions.